Bloom's
GUIDES

Albert Camus's
The Stranger

The Adventures of Huckleberry Finn

All the Pretty Horses

Animal Farm

The Autobiography of Malcolm X

The Awakening

Beloved

Beowulf

Brave New World

The Canterbury Tales

The Catcher in the Rye

The Chosen

The Crucible

Cry, the Beloved Country

Death of a Salesman

Fahrenheit 451

Frankenstein

The Glass Menagerie

The Grapes of Wrath

Great Expectations

The Great Gatsby

Hamlet

The Handmaid's Tale

The House on Mango Street

I Know Why the Caged Bird Sings

The Iliad

Invisible Man

Jane Eyre

Lord of the Flies

Macbeth

Maggie: A Girl of the Streets

The Member of the Wedding

The Metamorphosis

Native Son

1984

The Odyssey

Oedipus Rex

Of Mice and Men

One Hundred Years of Solitude

Pride and Prejudice

Ragtime

The Red Badge of Courage

Romeo and Juliet

The Scarlet Letter

A Separate Peace

Slaughterhouse-Five

Snow Falling on Cedars

The Stranger

A Streetcar Named Desire

The Sun Also Rises

A Tale of Two Cities

The Things They Carried

To Kill a Mockingbird

Uncle Tom's Cabin

The Waste Land

Wuthering Heights

Bloom's
GUIDES

Albert Camus's
The Stranger

Edited & with an Introduction
by Harold Bloom

BLOOM'S
LITERARY CRITICISM
An imprint of Infobase Publishing

Bloom's Guides: The Stranger

Copyright © 2008 by Infobase Publishing

Introduction © 2008 by Harold Bloom

Bloom's Literary Criticism
An imprint of Infobase Publishing
132 West 31st Street
New York, NY 10001

Library of Congress Cataloging-in-Publication Data
Albert Camus's The stranger / [edited by] Harold Bloom.
    p. cm. — (Bloom's guides)
  Includes bibliographical references and index.
  ISBN 978-0-7910-9829-5 (hardcover)
  1. Camus, Albert, 1913–1960. Étranger. I. Bloom, Harold. II. Title.
III. Series.

PQ2605.A3734E8335 2008
843'.914—dc22

                                    2007047571

Contributing Editor: Pamela Loos
Cover design by Takeshi Takahashi
Printed in the United States of America
Bang EJB 10 9 8 7 6 5 4 3 2 1
This book is printed on acid-free paper.

Contents

Introduction

HAROLD BLOOM

Albert Camus wrote and published *L'Etranger* before he was thirty. Only forty-six when he was killed in a car crash, Camus might seem an unfulfilled novelist, except that he was always essentially an essayist, even in his narrative fictions. *The Stranger* inflicts a considerable wound at first reading. I have just reread it after many years and am a touch saddened by its imaginative inadequacy, yet remain moved by its protagonist's pragmatic innocence. Meursault may be an odd version of Voltaire's Candide, but Jean Paul Sartre's insight remains correct, and *The Stranger*, no comedy, clearly has its affinity with Voltaire's "philosophical" fables, *Candide* and *Zadig*. An emblematic rather than enigmatic figure, Meursault compares poorly with Dostoevsky's fierce nihilists or with Kafka's guilty obsessives. An admirer of Melville and of Faulkner, Camus could not begin to match the terrifying Shakespearean inwardness of Captain Ahab or of Darl Bundren (*As I Lay Dying*). Lucid, severe, and engaging, *The Stranger* nevertheless is a tendentious work, one that knows too well what it is about and what its effect upon the reader will be.

"We have to labor and to struggle to reconquer solitude." That is Camus in his *Notebooks* in September 1937, when he was going on twenty-four. We need not consider Camus the most authentic spokesman of aesthetic solitude in the century just past—that distinction belongs to Franz Kafka, rightly considered by W.H. Auden to have been the Dante of his age. Kafka, desperate for happiness, found next to none. Camus, who thought of himself as happy, can seem a minor moralist when compared to Kafka or to Freud. And yet Camus became the most representative intellectual of the 1950s, both in France and throughout the West. He stood for individualism—moral, aesthetic, social, political—and for the ultimate value of each person's consciousness, however absurd (or absurdist) such consciousness might be.

And yet time has dimmed Camus, particularly as a literary artist. Almost fifty years after his death, we read him as an incarnation of the 1950s, not as a seer of eternity like Kafka or like Samuel Beckett. On the scale of a James Joyce or a Marcel Proust, Camus's fictions fade out of existence. Is Camus now more than a nostalgia, and is *The Stranger* still a poignant and persuasive narrative? A period piece can have its own value, but time will at last efface it.

I first read *The Stranger* in 1948, when I was eighteen, and was strongly moved. Returning to it in 1988, I was rather disappointed; time seemed to have worn it smooth. Reading it now a third time, I find I hover between my two earlier critical impressions. The book's stance refreshes me, as it did not twelve years ago, even though I cannot recapture the curious vividness *The Stranger* seemed to possess more than a half century back. *Then* it seemed tragic, though on a minor scale, an aesthetic dignity I could not locate in 1988. Tragedy, today, clearly is too large a notion to apply to Meursault. Camus regards him as essentially innocent, but if Meursault is nature's victim, or society's, rather than of some element in his self, then who would think him tragic? And yet Camus presents Meursault, extreme though he be, as a valid self, one that ought to survive. This is a subtle test for the reader, since Meursault is just barely sympathetic. At first, indeed, Meursault's is an inadequate consciousness as, dazed by the North African sun, Meursault murders a man, gratuitously, and evidently without willing himself to do so. Though he never feels, or expresses, remorse for the murder, Meursault changes as he undergoes legal judgment and approaches execution. Everything had been all the same to Meursault; he had seemed incapable of wanting anything very much, or wanting it more than another thing. As he awaits death, Meursault affirms a version of self: the knowing pariah who wants only the enmity of the state and the people.

Camus makes Meursault into someone we are in no position to judge, but that is an aesthetic risk, because can we still care when we are not competent to at least reach for judgment? Christianity is massively irrelevant to *The Stranger*, and to all of Camus's work. Secular humanism, now out of fashion, is affirmed throughout Camus, and today I am touched by the desperate minimalism of Meursault. To see that even Meursault ought to be allowed to go on is to see again the obscenity of capital punishment. The United States, these days, executes on a fairly grand scale. Today, *The Stranger* ironically becomes a strong parable against the death penalty. Meursault is not as yet an impressive person as his book closes, but he *has* begun to change, to feel, to choose, to will. To destroy him is more than a societal blunder, in Camus's view. Meursault's life has been an absurdity, but to take away his life is even more absurd.

# Biographical Sketch

Albert Camus was born on November 7, 1913, in eastern Algeria, which was then a territory of France. His father was Lucien Auguste Camus, a supervisor at a vineyard, who was of French ancestry. His mother was Catherine-Hélène Sintès Camus, of Spanish heritage. She was almost entirely deaf and was illiterate. Aside from Albert, the couple had another son, Lucien, who was born in 1910.

In 1914 Lucien Auguste Camus was called to serve in World War I, was wounded, and died that same year. Catherine-Hélène and her children moved in with her mother and brother in Algiers. Despite the family's relative destitution and an often tyrannical grandmother, Albert referred to his childhood as happy and made friends easily. In 1930, while still in high school, he was diagnosed with tuberculosis and forced to drop out. He returned to finish, though, and later, in 1933, started attending the University of Algiers. In 1934 he married Simone Hié, a young woman addicted to morphine; by fall 1937 they had separated, and in 1940 they divorced.

In 1937 Camus's first work, *L'Envers et l'endroit* (*The Wrong Side and the Right Side*), a book of short writings, was published. He then took a job as a journalist, moving to Paris when the paper he worked for ceased publication. He soon found employment at another paper. In 1940 he married Francine Faure, who had also lost her father in World War I and whose mother was not keen on having Camus as a son-in-law. By 1942 Camus's first novel, *L'Étranger* (*The Stranger*), was published as well as *Le mythe de Sisyphe* (*The Myth of Sisyphus*), a philosophical essay that addressed some of the concepts from his novel. Jean-Paul Sartre, Andre Malraux, and others commented on the great merit of the novel, while philosophers (later including Sartre and Simone de Beauvoir) and others attacked *Sisyphe*. Despite the varying receptions, from these two works, Camus gained celebrity status.

In 1943 Camus moved to Paris, where he worked for the publisher Gallimard and helped produce the newspaper *Combat*, a publication associated with the underground Resistance and that he later became editor of until 1947. Once Paris was liberated in 1944, the newspaper was published openly and viewed as the foremost opinion journal. During this time, Camus was a notable figure in the French existentialist circle that included Sartre, Beauvoir, and others. In 1945 the Camus's twins, Jean and Catherine, were born.

Also in the mid-1940s, Camus had two plays produced and published. *Le Malentendu* (*Cross Purpose*) was performed in 1944 and *Caligula* in 1945, with the latter receiving an enthusiastic response. Camus viewed this play, along with *L'Étranger* and *Sisyphe*, as belonging to his absurd works, which he saw as his first stage of thought. Also in 1947, a second novel, *La Peste* (*The Plague*), was published and received a mixed response. Camus saw this work as part of his second stage, which was concerned with humanism.

In 1948 Camus produced *L'Etat de siège* (*State of Siege*), which he referred to as a morality play similar to those of medieval times. The work addressed ideas similar to the ones explored in *The Plague*, yet the play was a failure. Not long after its run, Camus produced, in 1949, *Les Juste* (*The Just Assassins*), which was based on revolutionary activities that had taken place in Russia in 1905. Aside from creating these plays, Camus adapted several plays for the stage. During the 1950s, he hoped to become even more engrossed in the stage and tried to become a director of his own theater.

Camus's *L'Homme révolté* (*The Rebel*) was a long essay that covered some of the ideas explored in *La Peste*. It was published in 1951, and Camus viewed it as belonging to his second stage of thought as well. The work gained much attention in France and led to a confrontation between Camus and Sartre that permanently left them at odds. In the text, Camus pointed out the harm caused by revolution, whereas Sartre had been advocating joining forces with communists.

Camus's next major text was *La Chute* (*The Fall*), a novel that was published in 1956 and may be seen as resulting from his own feelings of alienation from his wife and from members of the intellectual community because of his political views.

In 1957 he published his collection of short fiction, *L'Exil et le royaume* (*Exile and the Kingdom*), thematically focused on separation and the impossibility of communicating. That same year he was awarded the Nobel Prize for Literature. In late 1959 and early 1960 Camus was working on a novel and was to become director of a Paris theater, but on January 4 he was killed in a car accident. The manuscript for *Le Premier Homme* (*The First Man*) was with him in the car and later published.

The Story Behind the Story

The Stranger was found greatly appealing when it was first published, and for many years after, young readers in particular saw it as addressing their plight. While *The Stranger* was published when World War II was in progress, Camus actually had been working on the title and its key ideas much earlier. When he first took up the notion of the work, the world already had suffered excessively from World War I. While all had not been so ideal before World War I, the end of the conflict left people feeling that the world was horrific and incomprehensible and that technology could be a force not just of advancement but of destruction. For Camus the war had a personal toll, claiming his father and reducing his family's circumstances as a result.

World War II occurred not long after the conclusion of the century's first major conflict. Hitler's rise brought with it the stark realization of evil's existence and showed that seemingly average men could be convinced to commit atrocities. Camus was still a relatively young man when Germans moved into France during the war. (He had been born in Algeria when it was a French territory, was of partial French heritage, and had also lived in France.) For many, the world appeared chaotic and unfathomable. People wondered how to go on but knew they must. *The Stranger* and other works of Camus addressed this despair and what comes from it.

In *The Stranger*, Camus creates a fiction that expresses his key concept—the absurd. This notion seemed to speak directly to the historical period in which the book was initially published. At the same time, the novel stood not just as a response to the horrors of expansive wars but as a vision of the timeless struggle of individuals making their way through life. More specifically, the absurdist idea is that people live in a universe that has no meaning, despite an intense human desire for meaning to exist. In Camus's view, individuals must come to recognize that this is the situation; with this recognition, people can then move to a new state, happy, despite the grim realities of the situation.

In *The Stranger*, the world of the protagonist expresses Camus's view of the absurd. The protagonist, Meursault, continually states that things do not matter, not only to him personally but in the world at large. In short, while people around him feel the world has some innate logic guiding it, Meursault does not see it that way. This perspective is what leads him to say, for example, that working in Paris or getting married really has no significance.

The confrontation between Meursault's view and that of nearly everyone else occurs when he is arrested and put on trial. Since Meursault shows no remorse for killing the Arab and has no real explanation for why he did it in the first place, much less why he fired so many shots, the prosecutor and others piece together their own conclusion. They insist on a logical explanation, even though their logic may be flawed or wrong. Their faulty thinking leads them to believe that Meursault has no morals and deserves the greatest punishment possible, the death penalty. Ironically, while Meursault kills the Arab and is seen as despicable, society kills Meursault and feels this is the proper response. A similar twist, in terms of violence, occurs earlier in the novel when the police come to Raymond's door because he is beating his girlfriend, and the police, in turn, slap Raymond for his behavior.

Meursault is pushed near his breaking point when he is condemned to death and the chaplain at the jail tries to turn him to God. Meursault insists he will not become a believer, though. After his outburst with the priest, Meursault realizes that the world is indifferent but, despite this conclusion, he has been happy and will continue to be.

While Camus presented his absurdist perspective in *The Stranger*, he explains it more directly in his essay *The Myth of Sisyphus*. Sisyphus is condemned to the intense labor of pushing a huge stone up a hill. When he finally is able to reach the top, the stone naturally rolls back down again, and the process must begin again. Despite the recurring cycle of unending labor he is subjected to, for Camus, Sisyphus is happy in his labor; there is pleasure in struggle. Camus imported this absurdist perspective to his play *Caligula*, which he also worked on when he was writing *Sisyphus* and *Stranger*.

In yet another work, his novel *The Plague* (*La Peste*), Camus also assumes an absurdist viewpoint, yet rather than the work being about the individual facing the world's indifference, in *The Plague*, when sickness strikes, all of humanity is vulnerable and must face the world's indifference. Rather than humanity becoming ruthless, though, people recognize that their friends and families are of utmost importance, and they help other individuals in need as well. After the threat has passed, though, people return to their previous self-centered state. Camus was not a writer invested in happy endings.

List of Characters

Meursault is the young man who is the novel's protagonist and first-person narrator. He is a conscientious clerk in an office in Algiers. He lived in a small flat with his mother but then moved her to an elder-care facility. After her move, he shifted all his furniture, which is mostly shabby, into one room so he would not have to take care of the other rooms. He is a great observer of people and his surroundings. He says little and seems to have no awareness of his feelings. He believes almost nothing matters and does not believe in God. Only right before his death does he come to recognize that the world is indifferent but that such a state does not matter, as he has been happy despite it.

Madame Meursault's death is the first event we learn about when the book opens. She is the mother of the protagonist. She and her son have not had the best or closest relationship, he writes. When she initially moves into the retirement home, she cries often, but, her son writes, once she has been there for a while, she does not ever want to leave. Meursault finds out at her funeral that she had developed a close relationship with Thomas Pérez, a man who also lives at the facility. She also has another good friend there, who weeps intensely at her vigil. While for much of the book Meursault seems to have had a poor relationship with his mother, at various points late in the narrative, he remembers things about his mother that seem to provide him some form of comfort.

Thomas Pérez lives at the retirement home where he had established a close relationship with Madame Meursault. He is the one person from the facility who is allowed to attend her funeral. He falls behind the others in the funeral procession but knows the area and so takes shortcuts to keep from falling even farther behind. His face is wet with tears at the funeral, where he eventually faints. He does not speak to Meursault at the service but later is called to testify against him in court.

Masson is Raymond's friend who owns a bungalow at the beach and invites Raymond, Meursault, and Marie to visit there. Masson takes a liking to Meursault. The three men even discuss staying together at the beach house for a month. Masson follows Raymond's directions about dealing with the Arabs and shows himself to be a strong fighter.

Marie Cardona is a secretary who had worked for a short time in the office where Meursault works. She runs into Meursault the day after his mother's funeral, and immediately the two hit it off. Despite the fact that Meursault is still in official mourning when he meets Marie, they enjoy the day together, go to a comic film, and sleep together. Marie is the most joyous character in the text; she laughs often, and Meursault finds her attractive. Marie wants to marry Meursault even after he twice tells her he probably does not love her. She seems to not understand him but thinks that her curiosity about him may be what attracts her to him, although she admits that she could also turn against him.

Raymond Sintès is another of Meursault's neighbors. He says he works in a warehouse and is quite distressed that people say he works as a pimp. He admits that he is hot tempered. He looks to Meursault for advice and help. Meursault agrees to write a letter to Raymond's girlfriend, part of Raymond's plan to get revenge on her for cheating on him. Raymond tells Meursault that he will be his pal. Raymond beats his girlfriend as well as her brother. Later, he testifies on Meursault's behalf. The prosecutor, though, uses as part of his case against Meursault the fact that Meursault is a friend of Raymond, a person with such a questionable background.

Céleste owns a restaurant that Meursault frequents. Meursault thinks of him as a good person. Céleste is concerned with how Salamano mistreats his dog and is sympathetic when Meursault's mother dies. Céleste earnestly tries to help Meursault; Céleste testifies at the trial and calls Merusault a friend.

Salamano is Meursault's neighbor. Initially, Meursault relates how the man brutalizes his dog. Later, when the man loses his dog, he becomes upset, and a different perspective on his character is revealed. He, like Meursault, is a man judged harshly by society. Salamano testifies at Meursault's trial on his neighbor's behalf.

Emmanuel works in the office where Meursault is employed. Emmanuel lends Meursault items for mourning. Emmanuel also has fun with Meursault: they jump on the back of a truck for a free ride, eat together, and see films together. At the movies, Meursault often explains things to Emmanuel; apparently, Emmanuel, like other characters in the book, is not as intelligent or perceptive as Meursault is.

The **Arabs** follow Raymond because he has beaten one of the men's sister. Raymond believed the woman cheated on him, and so he beat her as part of his plan to get revenge. Raymond gets in a fight with the woman's brother, and then the brother and his friend follow Raymond to the beach, where another fight ensues, and Meursault ends up killing the brother. While several characters are not noted by name in the text but referred to by their occupation ("the prosecutor," for instance), the Arabs are the only ones generically referred to solely by their ethnicity.

The **chaplain** manages to visit Meursault in his cell, even though Meursault has repeatedly turned down his requests to do so. The chaplain is kind and cannot fathom that Meursault does not believe in God and can be so thoroughly hardhearted. The chaplain's insistence on questioning Meursault and his resignation that all he can do is to pray for him causes Meursault to come to new realizations, seemingly at the end of his life.

The **doorkeeper** at the old-age facility had originally moved to the center as a resident. He then took on the responsibility of being doorkeeper and no longer considers himself one of the inhabitants there. He seems understanding when Meursault does not want to see his mother's body and when Meursault wants him to stay and keep him company. The doorkeeper says Meursault should eat, but when Meursault does not want to, the man gets him coffee instead. He and Meursault also share cigarettes in the room containing Meursault's dead mother. At Meursault's trial, however, the doorkeeper gives testimony that makes Meursault seem unfeeling.

The **employer** is Meursault's boss. From Meursault's perspective, the boss enforces the rules. For instance, the boss is seemingly annoyed that Meursault needs time off for his mother's funeral (although later he seems more understanding), and Meursault worries about taking a personal call at work because the employer will be annoyed that Meursault is wasting time. The employer asks Meursault if he would like to work in a new office in Paris, and when Meursault is not receptive to the promotion, the employer is irritated at his lack of ambition.

The **examining magistrate** questions Meursault after he kills the Arab. The magistrate insists on knowing why Meursault fired one shot, paused, and then fired additional rounds. When Meursault can give him no answer, the magistrate becomes more frustrated and talks to Meursault about God. The magistrate is more distressed when Meursault says he does not believe in God. The magistrate says that all men in jail break down when they see the crucifix, so he is confounded when Meursault does not. Later, the magistrate labels Meursault "Mr. Antichrist."

The **lawyer** is appointed to defend Meursault. He is young, says he has studied Meursault's case intensely, and advises Meursault not to talk at the trial. When the lawyer initially questions Meursault, the lawyer realizes that Meursault's unusual reactions will not sit well with the judges and jury. Still, the lawyer is no match for the prosecutor. At times, people in the courtroom laugh at the lawyer, and he seems to misread how the trial is going (unless he correctly assesses the course of the trial but just lies about it to Meursault).

The **prosecutor** works hard to get the jury to believe not only that Meursault is guilty of murder but that he deserves to be put to death. The prosecutor focuses particular attention on Meursault's seemingly unfeeling manner at his mother's funeral, arguing that the apparent lack of emotion shows the kind of heartless man Meursault really is. The prosecutor even insits that Meursault is also guilty in the parricide case that follows his trial.

The **robot woman** is given this name by Meursault. Once when he is dining at Céleste's, she sits with him, and he carefully observes her unusual behavior. Even before she receives her meal, she determines how much it will cost and gets the money out of her purse. She intently examines a radio magazine, marking it up as she goes through it. After she leaves, Meursault follows her a bit because he finds her so odd. Later, at his trial, she is there and intently observes him. Her presence serves as a subtle suggestion that even a minor encounter can affect one's future.

The **warden** runs the retirement facility. He understands that Meursault could no longer take care of his mother and so sent her to live at the center. The warden is in charge of the arrangements related to the vigil and funeral and exerts a certain amount of control over the people who live at the home, partially because managing certain affairs makes things easier for the workers. The warden attends the procession and funeral. Before the procession starts, he tells Meursault about his mother's close relationship with Pérez. The warden does not introduce the two men, however. Later, at Meursault's trial, the warden testifies about Meursault's lack of emotion.

Summary and Analysis

The novel opens with an unemotional announcement by the first-person narrator. He tells the reader, directly, flatly, that his mother has died that day. Rather than describing his feelings, he is concerned instead with whether she really died that day or the day before. He describes the telegram that gave him the news. The telegram mimics his own seeming lack of emotion, yet from a telegram a short, brief, unemotional statement is expected, while from a son whose mother has just died, a similar tone is not. The writer of the telegram acknowledges that the announcement is one that will provoke emotion. The author of the telegram offers sympathy, although there is a coldness even in that, since we are not told the identity of the person who sent the telegram, just that it came from the old-age home where the narrator's mother had lived.

From here the narrator gives details about getting to the home. It is in Marengo, some 50 miles from Algiers. The narrator plans to take a bus there, spend the night, and be back the following evening. He has told his employer he needs two days off, and he believes the employer was annoyed. The narrator apologized to the boss and said, "it's not my fault, you know," an unusual comment, since the boss must be annoyed that his worker will miss two days but obviously knows the situation is not the employee's fault. The narrator thinks that it has not really sunk in with the employer that someone has died, and the narrator admits that for him it is as if his mother has not died either.

Before catching his bus, the narrator eats at Celeste's restaurant, a place where he goes so often the people there know him; those gathered there offer sympathy. He borrows a black tie and a mourning band from Emmanuel, who is most likely a friend or an acquaintance. It is very hot, and the narrator rushes off to catch the bus and then sleeps during the ride.

At the home, the narrator asks to see his mother at once but is told he must wait for the warden. When the warden arrives, he refers to the dead mother as "Madame Meursault" and tells the narrator, whom he calls "my boy," that he understands that he did not have the money to "see that she was properly cared for." This is a curious comment, since the warden is the one in charge of the care provided at the home, we assume, and yet willingly acknowledges its seeming inadequacy.

We learn that the narrator does not make much money. The warden says Madame Meursault was happier at the home than she would have been living with her son and that she had good friends there. The narrator thinks to himself that the warden is right, that his mother was not happy living with him, and that while she cried when she first moved to the facility, in time she did not ever want to leave. The narrator says this is part of the reason why he seldom visited her in the past year, although this hardly seems a logical excuse. He relates the difficulties entailed in getting to the home as well, offering more reasons why he did not visit much.

The warden has continued talking, but the narrator says he was not paying much attention, a response elicited from him several other times in the novel. The response shows his lack of interest and his passive acceptance of situations, since he usually does not stop people from talking, even when he is no longer interested in what they are saying. The warden asks the narrator if he would like to see his mother. The narrator does not answer; a similar unresponsive silence occurs several times in the novel. It seems another indication of the narrator existing in his own world, unconcerned with others' needs for answers and unconcerned with following accepted etiquette.

The warden tells the narrator his mother has been moved to a small mortuary, because it is upsetting to the others who live at the care facility when someone dies and, in turn, causes extra troubles for the staff. The remark echoes the narrator's own selfish comment about the trouble entailed in coming to visit his mother. The narrator keeps his thoughts to himself, whereas the warden expresses his concern with things going smoothly over his concern for people's need to mourn. For him, old people, or perhaps people overall, seem to be too much trouble.

The warden takes "Monsieur Meursault" to the mortuary. In the book, we never learn the narrator's first name, making him seem less of an individual. Even his surname is rarely used. The warden says the funeral will be the following morning and that Madame Meursault's friends said she wanted a religious ceremony. Meursault thanks the warden. He then tells the reader that he thought his mother was not religious. He does not point this out to the warden, though, and we wonder if Meursault does not truly know his mother or if it is his mother's friends who do not know her well. As the novel progresses, religion emerges as a sign of society's insistence on following a designated path that is commonly believed to offer hope and redemption. Here Meursault says nothing about religion, but at the book's conclusion, he defiantly rails against a priest. At this part of the text, the brief references to religion are a minor preparation for what is to come.

When the narrator enters the mortuary, the first things he notices are not the coffin with his mother inside but how bright and clean the room is and the furniture it contains. Again, this is an unexpected observation. As the book progresses, the narrator's continued attention to light and the physical realm as well as his almost complete lack of emotion emerge more pointedly.

The doorkeeper rushes in to open the coffin so Meursault can see his mother, but Meursault says he does not want to see her. He is then embarrassed, because he realizes it was not what he was supposed to say, but the keeper seems to accept this, even when Meursault says he really does not know why he does not want to see her. When the keeper goes to leave, he realizes Meursault actually wants him to stay, which he does, becoming more talkative. One of the things he tells Meursault that the young man finds interesting is that, because of the heat, bodies must be buried quickly in this area, whereas in Paris such a rush is not necessary. Again, Meursault is interested in the physical, specifically the power of the heat. Paris, too, will come up again later as a point of contrast.

The doorkeeper says Meursault should have something to eat, but he says he is not hungry, and the doorkeeper offers him a cup of coffee instead. Meursault drinks it and wishes he could have a cigarette as well but wonders if it is proper to do so, considering the circumstances. He decides smoking should not matter, though, and offers the doorkeeper a cigarette as well, and they both smoke. The bright lights in the room bother Meursault so much that he asks if some of them can be turned off. The doorkeeper says they can only be all on or all off. When the other mourners enter the room later, they are not bothered by the lights as Meursault is.

The doorkeeper says that the friends of Meursault's mother will soon be arriving to hold a vigil through the night, and he goes to get them coffee. Meursault dozes and awakens to the bright light and to the sight of the friends entering. He observes them in great detail, and as they sit he tells the reader, "For a moment I had an absurd impression that they had come to sit in judgment on me." The remark is telling, since later in the book Meursault is indeed judged by people who, like these individuals, seem foreign to him.

One woman cries, and the doorkeeper tries to settle her down. He explains to Meursault that the woman was a great friend of his mother's. Meursault feels that his nerves are stressed by the other silent people in the room. They all have coffee, although most still sleep through the night. At dawn, Meursault is surprised that before the visitors leave each shakes his hand. They are following a tradition that implies an intimacy between them that Meursault feels is not actually there.

Meursault, the warden, and the undertaker's men prepare for the funeral. Again the warden asks Meursault if he wants to see his mother; this time Meursault directly declines the opportunity. The warden tells Meursault that others who live at the home are not allowed to go to such funerals, "to spare their feelings." However, one man is allowed to attend, Thomas Pérez, who was so close to the narrator's mother, others at the care facility used to joke about when the two would get married. The priest arrives as well as a woman who Meursault assumes is a nurse who works at the home. Pérez is there, too, and Meursault observes him carefully, yet the two do not speak.

As the group prepares to walk to the church in the funeral procession, the warden tells Meursault how Pérez and his mother would take long walks in the cool evenings. Meursault thinks he understands how his mother must have felt. Whereas the warden made the walks sound like a pleasant retreat, Meursault believes the evenings must have been "a mournful solace." In the hot morning sun, he feels "something inhuman" about the landscape. The procession starts, and Meursault notices that Pérez has a limp and starts to fall behind the others. A man in the group comments to Meursault on how hot it is and asks if the woman they are burying is Meursault's mother and how old she was. Meursault does not know her age, another indication of his indifference.

The heat is pervasive and intense. Meursault struggles as he walks. He realizes that Pérez knows the lay of the land so well that he frequently takes shortcuts so he will not fall too far behind. Meursault remembers little of the funeral but Pérez's tear-stained face. Meursault clearly remembers how Pérez looks but shows no sympathy for the man, even after he faints. Meursault remembers the red geraniums, the red earth, and the white roots amid the dirt that is thrown on the coffin. Later, on the bus home, he has a "little thrill of pleasure" as the bus nears his home and he imagines sleeping for many hours in his own bed.

In **chapter two**, Meursault wakes up on Saturday morning and realizes that he has a long weekend. He understands why his boss is annoyed: Meursault got two days off from work (four days when the weekend is counted), yet the funeral had occupied only Friday. Meursault says he can understand his employer's viewpoint. This shows Meursault as conscientious about his job and as someone who understands how society works. The thoughts also show severely skewed empathy, for while Meursault empathizes with his boss over a rather minor inconvenience, Meursault has shown no feeling for his mother losing her life or for his mother's friends at the home who are upset by the loss.

Meursault struggles to get up, noting that the previous day's "experiences" had been exhausting. He decides to go for a swim at the pool, where he sees many young people, among them Marie Cardona, a woman who had once worked for a short time as a typist at his office. He had liked her, and he believes she had liked him in return. He lounges with her on her raft in the pool. The sky is blue and gold, and when it gets too hot the two jump into the water. Marie appears to be enjoying Meursault's company as she laughs frequently. He asks her if she will go with him to the movies that evening, and she says she will if they can go to the comedy that everyone is buzzing about.

Marie sees that Meursault has a dark tie, and so she asks if he is in mourning. He says that his mother died the day before, even though the funeral was the day before and his mother had in fact died even earlier. Perhaps he felt she had died on the funeral day, though, because that was when he was with her for the last time. The answer, though, makes him seem even more unfeeling and imprecise. Meursault thinks that Marie is disturbed by the news, and he considers telling her the death was not his fault, the same words he had said to his employer. When Meursault had met with the warden, he had felt that the warden had somehow believed that Meursault was guilty. Apparently Meursault feels somehow responsible, perhaps for having to put his mother in an elder-care facility, perhaps for not visiting her more or taking care of her better, or perhaps for not feeling the way a proper mourner should. Or he does not even know what he feels guilty about.

Meursault and Marie go to the movie, and she spends the night at his place but is gone when he wakes up in the morning, having previously told him she had to meet her aunt. Meursault sleeps until ten and stays in bed until noon smoking cigarettes. He meanders through his small apartment, in which he has moved all the rather worn furniture into the bedroom because that one room is all he needs, and it spares him having to take care of the rest of his apartment. He reads an old newspaper and cuts out an ad that amuses him, more concerned with amusement than with keeping on top of the news.

He spends the rest of the day on his balcony, enjoying the fine weather and observing all the passersby who are hurrying along, while he is still and passively observant, surmising where they are going. People are out walking, others are on their way to and from the movies. The streets are quiet and then active again as people return from their various outings. Some animatedly talk of the movies they have seen; a team returns, jubilant from winning a game. Some of the team members yell up to Meursault, and some of the neighborhood women wave at him.

Meursault stays out until it is dark and quiet again, and only because he notices these changes does he realize it is getting late and that he should get something to eat. He fixes some food and remains inside, because the temperature has dropped considerably. He thinks about how he made it through another Sunday, his mother is buried, he will be going back to work, and nothing has really changed. His mother's burial is only one in a string of occurrences to which he remains indifferent.

Meursault returns to work when **chapter three** opens. His boss is in a good mood and asks if Meursault is tired and how old his mother was, the same question posed to Meursault earlier by the man at the funeral. Apparently this is a common query, and those asked are expected to know the answer. Meursault has no idea what his mother's age was, again showing how uninformed he is about his own mother.

Meursault observes how he enjoys washing his hands and drying them when the towel in the bathroom is still rather dry; at one point he had complained to his employer about how wet the towel is at the end of the day. The comment indicates again Meursault's concern with the physical. Additionally, it shows a certain inconsistency in how he lives, for while his own flat is in poor shape he expects the office to be held to a higher standard. This concern with so minor a detail also contrasts with what happens next in the chapter.

Meursault goes to lunch with Emmanuel, who works in another department in his office, and while they are out he and Emmanuel run to catch up with a truck, jump on, and get a free ride. The action seems carefree and exhilarating, not what a man concerned with the wetness of a towel would spontaneously do. The two men go to Céleste's for lunch, and

Céleste offers Meursault his sympathy at the loss of his mother. Céleste says he hopes Meursault is not feeling too badly, and Meursault answers "No," a response he will repeatedly give as the novel progresses, an answer opposite of what is commonly expected. Meursault takes a nap at his place, after drinking too much wine at lunch. He wakes, smokes a cigarette, returns to the stiflingly hot office, finishes his shift, and then enjoys the cool weather out by the wharves.

At his apartment building, Meursault runs into a neighbor, Salamano, and his mangy dog. While the dog and man have lived together for eight years, the two hate each other. Twice a day, at the same times each day, the two go for a walk that devolves into a confrontation. The dog pulls the man along, the man trips, he beats the dog, the dog cowers, then—the cycle renewing—the man drags the dog along again, the dog starts to tug against the leash, and the man beats the animal again. People who observe the behavior, such as Céleste, feel something should be done, but apparently no one has interfered. When Meursault tries to talk to Salamano on this occasion, the neighbor is too exasperated with the dog to even give a proper greeting.

Another neighbor, Raymond Sintès, enters. Most people believe he is a pimp, although he says he works in a warehouse. Meursault finds him interesting and thus is friendly with him. Raymond asks Meursault if he wants to have dinner with him and Meursault agrees, realizing he will not have to go through the trouble of cooking for himself. When Raymond turns on a light, Meursault sees that he has put a bandage around his hand, a grimy one, as befits the state of the room. Raymond explains that he got into a fight with a man and insists that he does not look for fights, although he has a short temper.

Raymond says he wants to ask Meursault's advice on something related to this fight. He promises they could be pals for life and asks if Meursault would like that, to which Meursault replies that he does not object to it, a noncommittal answer not unlike many he gives over the course of the novel. Raymond explains that the man he beat up is the brother of a woman Raymond is involved with. He quickly assures

Meursault that he knows people think he is a pimp but that that simply is not true.

Raymond explains his relationship with the woman. He has been paying all of her expenses and even gave her a little extra money, but she was not content with this. When he said she could get a job, she refused. He found clues that she was cheating on him, confronted her, and beat her. He admitted that it was not the first time he had physically abused her but that the other times were done "affectionately-like." Still, he felt this was not punishment enough, so he had asked some of his friends of questionable character what else he could do. On his own, though, he had come up with the idea of sending her a letter that would get her to repent. When she arrived at his place, he had taken her to bed then spit in her face and kicked her out.

At various points, Raymond asks Meursault what he thinks of the story, and Meursault responds at times in a noncommittal way and at times in agreement. Raymond asks Meursault to write the letter to the woman and he agrees, writing it on the spot, even though he has had a lot of wine. Raymond is happy with the letter and tells Meursault he knew he was "a brainy sort." Raymond asks if now they are pals. Meursault does not initially answer but eventually agrees when he sees how Raymond is so set on the idea.

It is late, and Meursault is tired. Raymond says that Meursault should not let things get to him and explains that he has heard that Meursault's mother died. He remarks that she was bound to die some day anyway, an insensitive and unsympathetic view of death that returns and is pondered at the end of the novel. Meursault leaves and lingers in the hallway, which he describes as dark as a grave. He hears Salamano's plaintive cry, "like a flower growing out of the silence and darkness"; somehow this bleak cry is seen as something fragrant and positive. Out of the negative, something good is still possible, a key idea that will inform the novel's conclusion and is heralded as well at the end of **chapter four**. This portion of the novel starts, though, with the narrator describing more leisure time. He goes to the movies with Emmanuel, a man with whom he is able to have fun. At times Meursault has to explain what the movie is about, and we realize that Emmanuel, like Raymond, is not as smart as Meursault. In fact, as the book progresses, we see that Meursault has no intellectually stimulating friends, fitting for a man who seems to not think about much of anything.

The narrator gives a lengthy description of his Saturday at a small beach with Marie. Late in the afternoon, the sun is not too hot, and the water is pleasant. Again, the two seem to thoroughly enjoy themselves. Marie teaches him a game to play in the water, and later they rush back to his apartment to be with each other.

Once there, they hear a woman in Raymond's room and hear Salamano yelling at his dog as he prepares to take him out for a walk. Meursault tells Marie about the relationship between the man and his dog, but while others have been disturbed by it, Marie laughs, which Meursault always finds enticing. Marie asks him if he loves her, and he answers by saying, "that sort of question had no meaning, really; but I supposed I didn't." Once again we see the narrator's lack of emotion. While it can be understandable that he does not love her, the first part of his answer is strange. To him the idea of loving or not loving has no meaning; he denies this part of life. Marie is disappointed by his answer, of course, but seems to return relatively quickly to her usual self.

Suddenly, a disturbance punctuates the afternoon. The couple hears Raymond fighting with a woman and then a horrific scream. A crowd immediately gathers in the hall. "Marie said, 'Wasn't it horrible!'" the narrator tells us, and as usual, he does not answer her. When she tells him to go for the police, he tells her he does not like law enforcement officials. His distaste for police officers is stronger than his desire to fulfill Marie's request.

The police arrive, and Raymond answers the door with a cigarette hanging from his lips. When the policeman tells him to take the cigarette out of his mouth, he does not, and the policeman slaps him, assaulting the man who coincidentally is in trouble for assaulting a woman. Ironically the very thing Raymond is in trouble for, assault, is what the policeman inflicts on him. This brief interlude of violence illustrates that there are different rules that apply to those in authority. The woman yells that Raymond is a pimp, and we wonder if this is true. He is shaking, hardly resembling the tough guy he makes himself out to be at other times in the book.

Later, Raymond goes to Meursault's apartment and tells him what happened. Meursault comments that Raymond taught the woman a lesson, what Raymond seemed to have wanted after all. Meursault appears undisturbed that the woman has been beaten and that Raymond is in trouble with the police as a result. Raymond agrees with Meursault's remark. He says he can handle the police but asks Meursault to go to the police and let them know that the woman had cheated on him; Meursault agrees. The two go out for a drink and a game of billiards, which Meursault seems to enjoy very much.

Back at the apartment, they find Salamano, disturbed because his dog has gotten out. Each of the other men tries to calm Salamano, giving him seemingly helpful information. Meursault, for instance, says the police have a pound for dogs and that Salamano's dog is probably there. All Salamano would need to do is pay a small fee to get the dog back. Salamano flies into a rage over the idea that he might have to pay to secure the return of such a miserable dog.

The three men part, but soon after, Salamano comes to Meursault's door, distressed that the police might actually keep the dog from him. Meursault reassures him that he should have no trouble getting his dog back. The man returns to his flat, and Meursault hears him apparently crying. Meursault states that this gets him thinking of his mother, although he does not know why and apparently only thinks of her briefly, since he has to get up early the next day. So Meursault goes to bed.

In **chapter five**, Meursault is at work and gets a phone call from Raymond, who invites him to his friend's home at the beach and says that his girlfriend's brother, along with some other Arabs, have been following him. Raymond asks Meursault to tell him if he sees the Arabs around their house later.

Meursault's employer calls him into his office, and Meursault feels uncomfortable because he assumes he has been summoned because he was on the phone with a friend and wasting time. It is curious that he feels "uneasy" over this when he has seemed so unfeeling in almost all other situations in which some emotional response would seem natural. Instead of chastising his employee, however, the boss tells Meursault he is thinking of opening an office in Paris and wants to know if Meursault would work there. From the boss's perspective, young men enjoy Paris, but Meursault responds that while he would go, he really does not care one way or the other. The boss is surprised, expecting that Meursault would find "a change of life" appealing, but Meursault says people's lives never really change.

The boss is annoyed and starts to chastise Meursault for his lack of drive. Meursault returns to his work and thinks of how he once had drive when he was a student but apparently lost that ambition once he left school. This is one of the few glimpses offered of Meursault's past, and it is only a limited impression at best. Why he left school is not revealed, but we now have some indication that Meursault's life has not been smooth, despite his claim that "it wasn't an unpleasant one." Even this is an odd characterization. He does not just say his life was pleasant but uses negative terms to characterize it, even though the description ultimately appears a positive one.

Marie comes to his apartment that evening and asks Meursault if he will marry her. He says he does not mind and will marry her if that is what she wants. She again asks him if he loves her, and he answers as he did when she first asked him—that it does not really matter but he supposes he does not. She says she does not understand why he would want to marry her then, and he answers that he will do it to make her happy. She says marriage is a serious thing, but he says that it is not. She says she wonders if she really loves him, and he answers matter of factly that he does not know the answer to that particular question. She calls him "a queer fellow," saying this may be why she loves him but also why she may come to hate him. This ties in with Salamano both loving and hating his dog and, to some degree, is reflected in Raymond turning against the woman he supposedly cared for. This dichotomy is present throughout Meursault's world and is perhaps the reason why he says so many things do not really matter.

Still, Marie says she wants to marry Meursault, and he responds that they should do so. He tells her his boss's idea about Paris, and she is excited and says she would love to go there. He tells her that he has been there, and he describes it negatively. They go for a walk, and she reveals that she has plans for the evening. She is surprised he does not ask her what the plans are, and she laughs at him.

Meursault has dinner at Céleste's, where an odd woman joins him. He watches her carefully as she studies the menu, determines how much her food will cost, and then digs the money from her purse. She studies a radio magazine and eats, all with robotlike movements, before leaving. Since Meursault has "nothing better to do," he follows her but finds he cannot keep up with her and so turns for home.

Once at home, Meursault meets Salamano in the hallway and invites him into his place. The man tells him his dog appears to be truly gone. Meursault finds Salamano boring, but because Meursault has nothing better to do, he keeps asking the man questions. We learn that the man got the dog when his wife died, because he had felt lonely even though he and his wife had not had the warmest marriage. Salamano calls the dog "cantankerous" but still a good companion and raves about how beautiful the dog's coat was before he got a skin disease. His coat had been his best feature, Salamano says, a transformation that again illustrates how changeable and inconsistent the world is. Salamano had taken great care of the dog to try to combat the skin disease.

Since Merusault seems to be getting tired, Salamano prepares to leave. He says Meursault's mother had liked the dog very much and that Meursault must be suffering greatly because of her death. The young man does not reply. Salamano says that people in the neighborhood spoke against Meursault because he had sent his mother to live in the old-age home. Salamano states, though, that he knew Meursault was devoted to her. Meursault is surprised that he had made such a bad impression on people. Salamano starts to leave and remarks on how difficult his life will be without his dog; his sensitivity shows even more when he says he hopes the neighborhood dogs do not bark that evening, as it makes him think his own dog is out there as well.

It is Sunday morning as **chapter six** opens. Meursault has a hard time waking up and does not feel well. Marie says he looks "like a mourner at a funeral," a curious description of a man who, when he attended his mother's funeral, seemed nothing like a typical mourner. Marie is her usual chipper self, and the two get Raymond and leave for the beach. Raymond, too, is cheerful, making Meursault's darker mood stand out all the more. Meursault's glum feelings and Marie's description of his funereal mood and mien are portents of tragic things to come.

The night before, Meursault had gone with Raymond to the police station and told them Raymond's girlfriend had cheated on him. In light of this, the police, who did not attempt to verify Meursault's testimony, let Raymond off with a warning.

As Marie, Raymond, and Meursault leave to catch the bus to the beach, they see the Arabs across the street looking at them. Once the three are on the bus, they are happy to see that the Arabs did not follow.

At the beach, it promises to be an exceptionally hot day. The three go to the bungalow owned by Raymond's friend Masson and his wife, whose name is not given, a notable omission as her husband's name is supplied. Other less important characters remain nameless as well—the Arabs, Raymond's girlfriend, and the warden, for example. Meursault himself is never given a first name, even though he is the protagonist. Only half a name may be fitting for a man who, for much of the book, seems to live a partial existence.

Meursault starts to perk up from being in the sun, and he and Masson join Marie in the water. Meursault feels even better when immersed in the cold water. Masson is the slower swimmer of the two men, so Meursault pushes ahead and catches up with Marie. They swim side by side, both of them "enjoying every moment." All three then go back to the beach, where Meursault falls asleep. Later, he is awakened by Marie, who tells him lunch must be ready. Marie and Meursault take one last swim, in which they delight.

Lunch is a feast, and Masson, Meursault, and probably Marie drink their share of the wine. After lunch, the three men go for a walk on the beach and notice two Arabs coming toward them. Raymond realizes one is his girlfriend's brother, the man who has been after him. The men keep coming closer, and the narrator notes that the sand is "as hot as fire." Raymond says that, if necessary, he will fight the man who is after him; he tells Masson to take care of the other man and Meursault to watch for others who might arrive on the scene. Raymond approaches the man who is after him and calls for Masson. Both men gain immediate advantages over the Arabs. Yet just when Raymond turns to brag to Meursault that he still has not finished fighting, the Arab takes out a knife and cuts Raymond in the arm and on the mouth. The Arabs flee, and Masson takes Raymond to a nearby doctor, while Meursault stays at the bungalow with the women.

Raymond returns in a sour mood. He says he is going for a walk and insists that no one go with him, but Meursault follows. It is outrageously hot. Meursault assumes Raymond has a specific destination in mind. They come to the end of the beach, marked by a large rock and a small stream, and find the two Arabs resting there. One blows on a reed and produces three notes repeatedly. Raymond asks Meursault if he should shoot them, but Meursault manages to talk him out of it and to get Raymond to give him the gun. Meursault thinks to himself that there would be no difference between firing and not firing. After some tense moments, the Arabs sneak away. Raymond and Meursault head back to the bungalow. Meursault thinks Raymond is happier, his friend starting to talk about the bus they will take home, already thinking about leaving the beach and the scene of the confrontations.

Raymond enters the house, but Meursault lags behind, distressed by the intense heat but also not wanting to go inside and be pleasant with the women. He thinks to himself that he could stay or go but that, either way, the end result would be nearly the same. This is almost the same thought he had earlier when he held Raymond's gun in his hand. The bleak notion is one that repeatedly surfaces in the book—that it does not matter whether or not one takes a new job, agrees to be someone's friend, or decides to get married. This philosophy, which others in the book have found exasperating when Meursault gives voice to it, does not seem to hold true by the end of the chapter. How different Meursault's life might have been had he not walked down the beach by himself.

Meursault feels as if he is battling the extreme heat and will not accept defeat. Meursault again arrives near the end of the beach and thinks of the cool shadow and silence by the rock, seeking refuge from the blazing heat and light and from a group of women crying at a bungalow. As he gets closer, he sees the Arab who was pursuing Raymond resting there. Meursault had assumed their confrontation was over and is surprised to find the man there. The two stare at each other, clutching the weapons they have in their pockets. Meursault is overwhelmed by the heat and reminded of how hot it was at his mother's funeral.

The Arab draws his knife and a flash of light reflects and glints from its surface. Sweat pours into Meursault's eyes, blinding him, and he feels the light from the knife "scarring my eyelashes, and gouging into my eyeballs." He shoots, an act that he knows in an instant has altered the whole day, a day when he had been so happy. It is a viewpoint that contrasts with his earlier insistence that actions do not matter. As the novel continues, we see that this new assessment proves true, at least in this case. The shooting matters very much. Meursault pauses and shoots four more times, even though the man was immobile.

In **chapter one of part two**, Meursault is questioned by the examining magistrate. The man asks Meursault if he has a lawyer, and Meursault answers that he does not and does not think he needs one since his case is "very simple." The magistrate smiles at Meursault's presumption. While earlier in the novel Meursault is considered the smart one whom people look to for answers, Meursault's judgment is often questionable from this point on. The magistrate tells him he will have a court-appointed lawyer, and Meursault remarks that this is a great benefit, almost as if he had not known about this right before, a lack of awareness that seems to contradict his portrayal as an intelligent and perceptive individual. Meursault is out of his element. This sense of dislocation is reinforced when he says he did not take the magistrate seriously at first. The magistrate starts to leave, and Meursault almost shakes hands with him; only then does Meursault remember killing the Arab.

The next day, Meursault's lawyer arrives to question him. The attorney is young yet says he has gone over the case with extreme care and should be able to exonerate Meursault if he follows the lawyer's instructions. The lawyer tells Meursault that investigators had learned from people at his mother's care facility that Meursault had appeared quite callous during her funeral. The lawyer says he must be able to counter this charge, so asks Meursault how he felt the day of the funeral.

Meursault explains that for some time he has been out of touch with his feelings. He says he was quite fond of his mother but adds that most people at some point wish the people they love were dead. The lawyer is distressed to hear this and tells Meursault he cannot speak like that to the magistrate or at the trial. The lawyer asks a few more questions about his apparent callousness but gets no response that will help him prepare Meursault's defense. The lawyer warns Meursault that he could be in serious trouble if some of the people who have spoken out against him testify at his trial.

Meursault says he does not understand the relevance of his mother's funeral to his shooting the Arab, and the lawyer states that this inability to connect or relate the events simply shows his client's lack of legal knowledge. This exchange echoes Meursault's earlier talk with the magistrate about his right to have a court-appointed lawyer. Meursault's characteristic ambivalence and lack of interest and awareness, whether genuine or feigned, seem to be catching up with him. The man who always seemed to have answers and to understand what was required now appears out of touch with the system. His prevailing attitude of indifference will work to his detriment in his present situation. Now Meursault realizes the lawyer is agitated by his answers. Meursault thinks of how to convey a better impression of himself, but says he feels too lazy to do so. His laziness did not seem to matter earlier, but in this setting, it will.

The same day, Meursault is again questioned by the magistrate. He asks Meursault again for his entire account of the killing, and by the end Meursault is tired from so much talking. The magistrate then changes the subject, asking if Meursault loved his mother. Meursault says, "Yes, like everybody else." He makes no comment about how the magistrate reacts but notes that the typist who was taking down his answers seemed to have made a mistake because he stops typing and fixes something he had previously typed. Meursault seems unaware that his answer is not very helpful to his case, despite his earlier meeting with his lawyer, where this issue was discussed at length.

Next the magistrate asks why Meursault shot the Arab four additional times after the initial bullet had struck the man. Meursault offers no answer, and although the magistrate keeps pressing the prisoner, Meursault remains silent. Frustrated, the magistrate takes a crucifix out of a drawer and tells Meursault that he believes in God and that anyone who is repentant can gain God's forgiveness. Meursault finds the magistrate's behavior alarming, even though he realizes he is in his current predicament because of his own rash and extreme actions. The room is very hot, and Meursault grows uncomfortable because flies keep landing on his cheeks. He realizes that the magistrate considers it important to know why Meursault fired the four extra shots. Meursault starts to tell him this aspect of the crime is of little importance, but the man interrupts him and asks if Meursault believes in God. Meursault says he does not, which only frustrates the magistrate further. He is baffled by Meursault and tells him that all the criminals he has dealt with have wept when they saw the crucifix.

Meursault is about to tell the magistrate that they cry because they are indeed criminals, but then he realizes that he is one, too, although he states that he never got used to that idea. The weary magistrate asks one last question—if Meursault feels badly about killing the Arab. Meursault answers that he feels vexed about it, and we know this is not what the magistrate wants to hear.

Meursault explains that for the next eleven months, the magistrate and his lawyer question him many times and that he has come to view them as family. He realizes this is "absurd" but then says how he enjoys when the magistrate pats him on the back and in a friendly tone calls him "Mr. Antichrist." Again, Meursault does not seem to understand what a serious situation he is in. While earlier in the novel his responses were at times bizarre, here his answers are self-destructively odd. For the most part, Meursault seems to be unaware of the full import of the situation he finds himself in.

In **chapter two of part two**, Meursault writes of his experience in prison. Initially, he had hoped for some great surprise or unexpected turn of events that would help him regain his freedom. That view changes, though, and he realizes his cell is where he is to stay when he gets a letter from Marie telling him that the prison rules prevent her from visiting him anymore because she is not his wife. This is another ironic revelation, since earlier he had thought it would not matter if they were married or not. From his cell, Meursault can catch tempting glimpses of the sea, but he remains cut off from the pools and beaches that had always been soothing and enjoyable places for him.

Marie is eventually allowed to visit once. Meursault is taken to a special room where other visitors are assembled. The place stands in contrast to his cell, as it is bright and white and full of voices. The prisoners are kept about 30 feet from the visitors, which means the people have to talk loudly. Meursault sees Marie smiling intensely. She speaks in a high-pitched voice and asks him if he is all right and has everything he wants. The first question is logical. The second seems almost mad, since what prisoner could possibly have everything he wants? Still, Meursault answers this positively, probably not wanting to upset Marie.

On one side of Meursault, a man is being visited by his wife, who talks quite loudly. The man and his wife seem rather at ease about his being in jail. On the other side of Meursault is a boy being visited by his mother, and the two do not talk. Marie says they must not lose hope, and Meursault agrees. She says Meursault will be acquitted and they will be able to get married and go swimming on Sundays. The woman visiting her husband loudly informs him that she has brought a basket for him and that he should check the contents to be sure nothing has been taken. They have experience with the system and stand in contrast to Marie and Meursault, who really do not know what to expect but wish to remain hopeful. The husband and wife also seem unlike the boy and his mother, who probably have little experience with prison since he is so young; they appear devastated by the young man's imprisonment.

The light is bothering Meursault, as is the loud woman's voice. Even here, after killing someone, for Meursault it is the physical realm that is disturbing, not his thoughts or emotions. One by one, the prisoners are led back to their cells. The room goes quiet when the first one is led away. It is after this visit that Meursault finds out he will get no more visits from Marie. He describes what his life is like in the prison and how his thinking has changed. At first he thought like "a free man" and that made life harder. He would think of things he used to be able to do, like go for a swim at the beach. The thought of that great pleasure no longer being possible only made life in prison worse. This phase of thinking like a free man lasted only a few months, he confesses.

Then Meursault starts thinking like a prisoner, noting the actual things he is able to do, such as go to the courtyard or get a visit from his lawyer. He explains that he ended up managing quite well and realizes that even if he had to live in a dead tree trunk he still would have been able to manage. He would get used to looking up at a bit of sky and at the birds that flew by. He thinks of how others have it worse than he does, and he thinks of how his mother used to say a person can get used to anything. This is the first time in the novel that he has had a thought about his mother other than those moments when others had asked about or mentioned her. While the idea he attributes to her is not unique, here it reflects a change, as he is thinking of her as someone who was a positive force in his life, while at all other points in the novel he seemed to be neutral about her or even to have found her a burden.

Meursault thinks of the other things that initially antagonized him in jail—not having sex or cigarettes. He becomes friendly with the chief jailer, who explains to him that people are kept in jail to be deprived of their liberty, so taking pleasures away from them is part of that process. This makes sense to Meursault. The man says Meursault is different from the other inmates because of his intelligence and mental abilities. This echoes a comment made about Meursault earlier in the novel, even though it seems Meursault is not really using his intelligence—one of his key attributes—in order to help himself.

Meursault explains that his problem in jail is how to kill time. One method he devises is memorizing and recalling objects in his cell. He learns to sleep longer, so it seems as if there is not as much time to get through. One day he finds a scrap of newspaper under his mattress and reads a report of a man who left his mother and sister, became rich, and decided to initially take on a fake identity when he went back to surprise them years later. They did not recognize him, and when they found out how much money he had, they killed him and took his money. Later, when they learned who he was, they killed themselves. Meursault comments on the story, saying the man brought this on himself by playing such a trick. From this statement, the reader can conclude that Meursault likewise has brought his situation on himself. He made friends with Raymond, a questionable character, took possession of Raymond's gun, did not realize the Arabs could still be nearby when he went to walk on his own, and then shot a man dead.

Meursault looks at his reflection and sees that he appears so serious, even when he tries to smile. He also hears his own voice and realizes he has been talking to himself for some time. The various parts that make him up seem foreign to and separate from him, as if he is not a unified consciousness in control of himself. He recalls what the nurse told him at his mother's funeral, that "there was no way out." At this point, he thinks of this only in terms of being stuck in prison; later the phrase will take on an additional connotation. This is a memory from his mother's funeral, an event that he has not thought about except when asked. Recalling his mother earlier and now thinking of her funeral seem to indicate a change may be taking place in Meursault.

In **chapter three of part two**, it is the day of Meursault's trial. His lawyer tells him the case should go quickly and that all the attention really will be focused on the case after his, a parricide, the murder of a parent or other close relative. Meursault is brought into the courtroom and comments to the police that he is not nervous but is interested in what will happen at the trial since he has never been at one before. The policeman tells him trials drag on for too long. Meursault notices a group of people staring at him intently. This reminds him of when one gets on a streetcar and the others already riding stare at you, hoping to amuse themselves, although he realizes these people make up the jury. Both of these instances, his comments to the police and his thoughts on the jury, show that his reactions are unusual and that he seems to not understand the gravity of his situation.

The air is stuffy in the courtroom, and many people are crowded inside, including numerous members of the press. One of the policemen knows someone from the press, who amiably comes over to chat. The reporter is kind to Meursault as well. He tells them there are so many journalists there because summer is a slow time for news. As a result, Meursault's case and the parricide that follows have been receiving a generous amount of coverage and attention.

The lawyers and judges enter. Meursault notices one journalist in particular, the youngest, who is staring at him intensely yet not showing any emotion. Meursault says, "For a moment I had an odd impression, as if I were being scrutinized by myself." This is a telling observation that ties in with the earlier instances of Meursault feeling distanced from his own reflection and voice. It also shows that even Meursault finds himself offputting. The judge calls for the witnesses to leave the room, and for the first time Meursault sees many people from his former existence, even the so-called "robot woman," who had sat with him once at Céleste's restaurant. The judge asks Meursault questions, and Meursault is aware of the robot woman and the young journalist watching him closely.

The judge says he has additional questions that might seem unrelated to the case but that are actually quite relevant. He asks why Meursault put his mother in a home and if doing so had caused any familial distress. Meursault explains that neither of them expected much of each other. The prosecutor asks if Meursault had intended to go and kill the Arab, and when Meursault says he had not, the prosecutor asks why, then, he went with a gun to the exact spot where he had seen the Arab earlier. Meursault replies that it was pure chance, to which the prosecutor responds in a "nasty tone."

The trial breaks for lunch. Meursault is rushed away and then returned for the trial's resumption. The room is even hotter by then, and Meursault says he was "barely conscious of where or who I was." We are reminded of his negative reactions to heat earlier in the book, especially when he killed the Arab. The heat and the persistent stares of the robot woman and the young journalist only add to the foreboding and oppressive atmosphere.

The warden from the retirement home testifies. At first, his remarks seem neutral, but then he adds that Meursault did not want to see his mother's body, did not cry at his mother's funeral, left immediately after it was done, and did not know his mother's age. The prosecutor appears triumphant, and Meursault states that he felt he could burst into tears and that he now realized that the people gathered loathed him. If the previously oblivious or willfully detached Meursault now sees trouble, he has surely grasped some of the direness of his situation.

The doorkeeper is then called to the stand and testifies that Meursault did not want to see his mother's body, had cigarettes and coffee at her vigil, and slept. Meursault's lawyer gets the doorkeeper to admit he had a cigarette as well. Meursault says the doorkeeper is telling the truth, and the prosecutor again appears triumphant.

Thomas Pérez is the next witness. He says that even though he had been a great friend of Meursault's mother, he only met Meursault at the funeral. Pérez admits that he was so taken with his own grief that he did not really pay attention to what Meursault was doing at the funeral. Meursault's lawyer plays this up, yet some people laugh at his questioning of Pérez. There is a break, and Meursault's lawyer tells him the case is going very well. We realize he is either delusional or deceitful.

Céleste comes to the stand and does his best to advocate for Meursault, but he is cut short by the judge and then, when given another opportunity to speak, seems to have almost nothing to add. As Céleste steps down from the witness stand, he looks extremely sorry that he could not have helped Meursault more, and Meursault states that he wanted to kiss a man for the first time in his life. Obviously, Meursault realizes he is in desperate straits. Earlier when he wrote at various points about kissing his girlfriend, it was not because of things she had done but usually because of how she looked. Now that his situation has changed, his perspective is changing as well. A kiss, for instance, becomes more meaningful.

Marie is called to the witness stand next. Meursault describes how she looks and also notes that she seems very nervous. The prosecutor gets her to say that her first date with Meursault occurred on the day after his mother's funeral. The prosecutor has her describe what they did on their date and gets her to admit that they saw a comic film. At this, the room goes silent. The prosecutor stands and gravely reminds the jury what they have just learned. Again there is complete silence, and then Marie bursts into tears. She tries to turn people in Meursault's favor, but then she is taken away.

Masson testifies next, followed by Salamano. While both have positive things to say about Meursault, no one seems to pay any attention to their testimonies, the narrator says. Following them on the witness stand is Raymond. He explains that the man who was killed was actually in a disagreement with him, not with Meursault. The prosecutor points out, though, that Meursault was the one who wrote the letter to the girlfriend that led to the killing. Raymond repeatedly argues that events occurred by chance, and the prosecutor points out how unlikely this is. He asks Raymond what he does for a living and then explains that Raymond really is not a warehouseman, as he claims, but a pimp. He says that Raymond and Meursault are close friends and describes Meursault as "an inhuman monster wholly without a moral sense."

Raymond and the defense lawyer object, but the prosecutor is allowed to continue. The prosecutor asks Raymond if he indeed is Meursault's friend. Raymond answers positively, and then the prosecutor asks Meursault if he is friends with Raymond. Meursault hesitates but answers in the affirmative. Earlier in the novel, when Raymond had asked Meursault if they were friends, Meursault had hesitated but then answered that they were, believing it would not matter what he said. That perspective, that little matters in life, now appears completely erroneous. For instance, witnesses that one would not expect to have any bearing on the murder have testified, showing how the apparently trivial and meaningless situations and exchanges involving them ultimately have mattered. Likewise, so many events have been brought up that would also seem to have no bearing on the killing, but the prosecutor is arguing that they are relevant. People and events now seem to matter very much to Meursault's fate.

The prosecutor makes a statement about Raymond, Meursault, and the events surrounding the case, declaring how despicable it was for Meursault to have acted the way he did the day after the funeral, how amoral the men are, and how sordid the killing was. The defense lawyer objects that the mother's death has nothing to do with the case, yet the prosecutor says they are indeed related, since how Meursault behaved at the funeral "showed he was already a criminal at heart." Meursault states that those in the room seemed to be greatly affected by these last words, that his lawyer was disturbed, and that even he "had a feeling things weren't going well."

We see that Meursault's response is again off target. In Meursault's own description of the trial, it seems to be going very poorly for him, yet he has a relatively minor reaction.

There is some change, though, in that this man who usually never mentions feelings has done so.

Meursault is brought back to his cell. During the trip he hears all the usual summer sounds "of a town I'd loved." Here he finally mentions love, although not for a person but for a place. During the ride he is exposed to all the physical sensations that brought him such pleasure as a free man. He realizes that all these everyday sounds can result in a blissful sleep at the end of the day (as he had experienced in his past) or be painful reminders for a man returning to a prison cell.

In **chapter four of part two**, the courtroom action resumes. Meursault, still not responding to the enormity of the events, observes that "it is always interesting" to hear others comment on one's character and conduct. He also remarks that there does not seem to be that much difference between the perspectives of the prosecutor and the defense lawyer. He describes as "irksome" the fact that he has not been speaking for himself during the trial but following his lawyer's direction to let the lawyer do the talking. Yet, when Meursault thinks further about this, he realizes he would have nothing to say anyway. He soon loses interest in listening to the prosecutor's boring closing arguments.

The prosecutor starts by giving his perspective on how Meursault handled his mother's death, insistent on tying that in with the killing of the Arab. Meursault notes a "shrewdness" about the prosecutor's argument. The prosecutor says that Meursault provoked the fight on the beach with the Arabs and later asked for Raymond's revolver, fully intending to go back and kill the Arab. Meursault shot five times because he wanted "to be certain of making a good job of it." The prosecutor argues that Meursault was fully aware of what he was doing when he killed the Arab and that he is an intelligent man.

Meursault contends that in most cases intelligence would be beneficial, yet here the prosecutor has used it against him. The lawyer also points out that Meursault has shown no remorse for his actions. Meursault thinks the prosecutor is right on this point, that he has never been able to regret anything and instead has always lived in the present or the immediate future. Meursault wishes he could, in "a quite friendly, almost affectionate way," explain this but notes that such a tone was not allowed in the courtroom. For an intelligent man, he does not seem to have grasped how he could best work within the system.

The prosecutor shows faulty logic. He admits that Meursault never had the moral qualities that others have and therefore should not be punished for this, but he adds that in criminal court there must be justice. He argues that Meursault is a danger to society. Then, in a frightening twist, he ties Meursault's case to the case of parricide that is to be tried next. The prosecutor says that Meursault, aside from being "morally guilty" of his mother's death, set a precedent for this next case and so is also guilty of that murder. The prosecutor asks that Meursault be found guilty and put to death.

The room is silent. Meursault is overcome by the heat and the prosecutor's words. The heat is the first irritant he mentions, again showing the priority he gives to the physical. The judge asks Meursault if he wants to speak and says he still does not understand his defense. Meursault tries to explain, but he admits that the explanation sounded nonsensical.

The next day the defense lawyer gives his closing arguments. Meursault writes that it "seemed interminable." Meursault is surprised to hear the lawyer use "I" as if he were Meursault when he is speaking. It is another instance of Meursault being distanced from the case. The lawyer is not as talented as the prosecutor, Meursault observes. This is another bad sign. The lawyer explains his vision of Meursault's soul, enumerating a string of positive attributes about the young man. Meursault feels everything becoming hazy. As the lawyer continues, Meursault recalls the sound of an ice cream vendor and other pleasures he no longer has access to. He realizes he is in a dire situation, and he feels like vomiting.

The heat is less intense since the day is drawing to a close. Those gathered wait for a verdict, but Meursault realizes the jury's decision is really only his concern. He looks around and notes that he has not tried to catch Marie's eye during the trial. He does so now but notes, "my heart seemed turned to stone, and I couldn't even return her smile." This is a bit surprising from a man who has been so distanced from his feelings.

Meursault is taken to a waiting room. His lawyer tells him he is confident all will go well. Then they are called back to the courtroom, and Meursault hears the pronouncement: he is condemned to death by beheading. When the judge asks him if he has something to say, he responds that he does not, again forgoing an opportunity to help himself.

Chapter five of part two opens with Meursault commenting that he has just refused to see the chaplain again, a reminder of when the magistrate pushed religion on Meursault earlier in his confinement. Meursault tries to keep the chaplain out, but society and its conventions prevail, and the chaplain shortly enters his cell.

Meursault thinks about how to prevent his execution. His new cell offers a thin glimpse of the sky. Earlier he had said he knew he could even get used to living in a dead tree, an adaptation that essentially describes his current situation. Only when he looks up can he see the world outside. He is managing this serious restriction because now his overwhelming concern is his own execution. Meursault wonders if anyone in his situation has managed to escape. He imagines making a dash for freedom but says he inevitably would be recaptured or shot in the back while trying.

Meursault thinks of a story his mother used to tell him about his father, who Meursault says he never had contact with. His mother would tell him of how his father was repulsed by execution but decided he needed to see one take place. After doing so, he was sickened. Meursault now feels that because nothing is more important than an execution, it should be of interest, although he had not thought that way before his own condemnation. He decides that if he ever regains his freedom, he will attend every execution. After thinking about this, Meursault realizes he is thinking about being free again, and he feels "a wild, absurd exaltation." He decides he cannot let his imagination fixate on freedom, though; the thought provokes an uncontrollable shivering fit.

Meursault goes back to thinking about how unfair the inevitability of dying is for a condemned man. He wishes there were a chance that the method of execution would not work. He thinks about how the guillotine functions and that a man condemned to be killed by this method actually wants the device to work properly. What a twist, he thinks, that the condemned should want his own death to go smoothly. Meursault also thinks of how he imagined the guillotine being a few steps above the ground. He realizes, though, that the condemned walks to the guillotine, which is on the same level as he is. Meursault is disappointed that there is no climbing up and away from the world. The killing is more discreet, efficient, and somewhat shameful, in his view.

Meursault knows that when one is executed, men come to take the condemned person at dawn. To avoid being surprised by this, Meursault changes his habits. He sleeps a bit during the day so he can be awake when dawn arrives. As each dawn approaches, he waits to hear footsteps coming toward his cell. Once dawn passes and no one comes for him, he experiences incredible relief, knowing he has at least twenty-four more hours to live. Again he thinks of his mother and how she would say that no matter how bad things were, there was always something to be thankful for. Though many people felt Meursault did not love his mother or treat her properly, here and at other points in the novel's concluding passages we see that Meursault is comforted by thoughts of her. When he thinks of her, the things he remembers are the typical lessons that mothers teach or impart to their children. Near the hour of his death, at least for a moment, he seems quite human after all.

Meursault also thinks about appealing his case. He imagines losing the appeal and tells himself that "it's common knowledge that life isn't worth living, anyhow." When this idea brings little comfort, he reasons that everyone has to die anyway and therefore it should not matter so much when that occurs. This brings no comfort. He thinks also that he could ultimately win his appeal. This idea brings an overwhelming joy, and he has to keep himself from getting too carried away about it.

Meursault also thinks about Marie, which he had not done in some time. He thinks about how he has not heard from her for such a long time and how she could, in fact, be dead. If so, he thinks, "her memory would mean nothing; I couldn't feel an interest in a dead girl." He realizes people would soon forget about him once he was dead. He does not get upset about this but recalls his mother's comment that people can get used to anything in time.

While earlier Meursault had imagined turning down a visit from the chaplain once again, now the chaplain just walks into his cell. To Meursault, the man is amiable enough. When the chaplain asks why Meursault has not wanted to see him, Meursault replies that he does not believe in God. The chaplain asks how Meursault can be so sure of this and tells Meursault that he has seen others like Meursault turn to God at this point in their lives.

The chaplain says he is convinced Meursault will win his appeal. This, though, does not make Meursault feel better, perhaps because he feels he cannot believe the man about God or anything else. The chaplain says that even though the appeal would be won, Meursault must work to relieve his enormous guilt. Meursault disagrees.

The chaplain explains that even the most wretched prisoners have seen the face of God in their cell walls. Meursault rejects this notion but admits that he has tried to see Marie's face in the wall, but such a vision has not materialized. The chaplain keeps trying to convince Meursault to believe in God and an afterlife, finally saying he will pray for Meursault whose "heart is hardened."

At this point, Meursault becomes angry. He yells at the chaplain and grabs him, spewing insults and saying the chaplain lives "like a corpse" while Meursault is completely sure of himself, of his life, and of his upcoming death. He says that nothing matters and that for his whole life a dark horizon has been in front of him. All people are condemned to die, and so nothing matters.

Jailers rush in to help the chaplain, who leaves with tears in his eyes. Meursault feels calm and so exhausted that he falls asleep. When he wakes, stars are shining on him, and he can hear and smell the summer night. He thinks of his mother and thinks he understands why she had such a close relationship with Thomas Pérez, whom the others called her fiancé, at the end of her life. Meursault thinks that it is at the very end when people feel free, "ready to start life all over again." He feels this way now, too. "I laid my heart open to the benign indifference of the universe. To feel it so like myself, indeed, so brotherly, made me realize that I'd been happy, and that I was happy still," he says. He ends by stating that on the day of his execution he hopes there will be a huge crowd of people who yell at him with loathing.

This man, who has seemed so indifferent to his own life, now sees the universe itself as indifferent. Rather than being distressed by this, he feels an affinity with the universe. He realizes, too, that happiness had been, and still is, a part of his life. This is quite a change from the man who throughout the text had expressed little or no feeling and claimed that he had been out of touch with his feelings for some time. Even though he realizes he is a part of a universe where there is no grand design leading to an everlasting reward, he sees that happiness, for him, existed and still does. The angry crowd at his execution cannot take away his happiness. He seems to wish for them to gather as proof of his assertions. Or perhaps they are symbolic of what he does not want to be; they make him happy to be a stranger after all.

Critical Views

JEAN-PAUL SARTRE ON CAMUS'S PORTRAYAL OF THE ABSURD

The absurd, to be sure, resides neither in man nor in the world, if you consider each separately. But since man's dominant characteristic is "being-in-the-world", the absurd is, in the end, an inseparable part of the human condition. Thus, the absurd is not, to begin with, *the object of a mere idea; it is revealed to us in a doleful illumination.* "Getting up, tram, four hours of work, meal, sleep, and Monday, Tuesday, Wednesday, Thursday, Friday, Saturday, in the same routine . . .",[1] and then, suddenly, "the setting collapses", and we find ourselves in a state of hopeless lucidity.

If we are able to refuse the misleading aid of religion or of existential philosophies, we then possess certain basic, obvious facts: the world is chaos, a "divine equivalence born of anarchy"; tomorrow does not exist, since we all die. "In a universe suddenly deprived of light and illusions, man feels himself an outsider. This exile is irrevocable, since he has no memories of a lost homeland and no hope of a promised land."[2] The reason is that man *is not* the world. "If I were a tree among other trees . . . this life would have a meaning, or rather this problem would have none, for I would be part of this world. I *would be* this world against which I set myself with my entire mind . . . It is preposterous reason which sets me against all creation."[3] This explains, in part, the title of our novel; the outsider is man confronting the world. M. Camus might as well have chosen the title of one of George Gissing's works, *Born in Exile.* The outsider is also man among men. "There are days when . . . you find that the person you've loved has become a stranger."[4] The stranger is, finally, myself in relation to myself, that is, natural man in relation to mind: "The stranger who, at certain moments, confronts us in a mirror."[5]

But that is not all; there is a *passion* of the absurd. The absurd man will not commit suicide; he wants to live, without relinquishing any of his certainty, without a future, without hope, without illusion and without resignation either. He stares at death with passionate attention and this fascination liberates him. He experiences the "divine irresponsibility" of the condemned man.

Since God does not exist and man dies, everything is permissible. One experience is as good as another; the important thing is simply to acquire as many as possible. "The ideal of the absurd man is the present and the succession of present moments before an ever-conscious spirit."[6] Confronted with this "quantitative ethic" all values collapse; thrown into this world, the absurd man, rebellious and irresponsible, has "nothing to justify". He is *innocent*, innocent as Somerset Maugham's savages before the arrival of the clergyman who teaches them Good and Evil, what is lawful and what is forbidden. For this man, *everything* is lawful. He is as innocent as Prince Mishkin, who "lives in an everlasting present, lightly tinged with smiles and indifference." Innocent in every sense of the word, he too is, if you like, an "Idiot".

And now we fully understand the title of Camus' novel. The outsider he wants to portray is precisely one of those terrible innocents who shock society by not accepting the rules of its game. He lives among outsiders, but to them, too, he is an outsider. That is why some people like him—for example, his mistress, Marie, who is fond of him "because he's odd". Others, like the courtroom crowd whose hatred he suddenly feels mounting towards him, hate him for the same reason. And we ourselves, who, on opening the book are not yet familiar with the feeling of the absurd, vainly try to judge him according to our usual standards. For us, too, he is an outsider.

Thus, the shock you felt when you opened the book and read, "I thought that here was another Sunday over with, that Mama was buried now, that I would go back to work again and that, on the whole, nothing had changed," was deliberate. It was the result of your first encounter with the absurd. But you probably hoped that as you progressed your uneasiness would fade, that everything would be slowly clarified, would be given a reasonable justification and explained. Your hopes were disappointed. *The Outsider* is not an explanatory book. The absurd man does not explain; he describes. Nor is it a book which proves anything. . . .

There is not a single unnecessary detail, not one that is not returned to later on and used in the argument. And when we close the book, we realize that it could not have had any other ending. In this world that has been stripped of its causality and presented as absurd, the smallest incident has weight. There is no single one which does not help to lead the hero to crime and capital punishment. *The Outsider* is a classical work, an orderly work, composed about the absurd and against the absurd. Is this quite what the author was aiming at? I do not know. I am simply presenting the reader's opinion.

How are we to classify this clear, dry work, so carefully composed beneath its seeming disorder, so "human", so open, too, once you have the key? It cannot be called a story, for a story explains and co-ordinates as it narrates. It substitutes the order of causality for chronological sequence. M. Camus calls it a "novel". The novel, however, requires continuous duration, development and the manifest presence of the irreversibility of time. I would hesitate somewhat to use the term "novel" for this succession of inert present moments which allows us to see, from underneath, the mechanical economy of something deliberately staged. Or, if it is a novel, it is so in the sense that *Zadig* and *Candide* are novels. It might be regarded as a moralist's short novel, one with a discreet touch of satire and a series of ironic portraits,[7] a novel that, for all the influence of the German existentialists and the American novelists, remains, at bottom, very close to the tales of Voltaire.

Notes

1. *The Myth of Sisyphus.*
2. *Ibid.*
3. *Ibid.*
4. *Ibid.*
5. *Ibid.*
6. *Ibid.*
7. Those of the pimp, the judge, the prosecuting attorney, etc.

R.W.B. Lewis on Camus's Style and Critique of Tragedy

Meursault tells his own story. Camus maintained later, during his debate with Sartre in *Les Temps Modernes*, that though *The Stranger* was written in the first person, it was "an exercise in objectivity and detachment," just as *The Plague*, written in the third person, was intended as the personal confession of Dr. Rieux. The sterile monotone of the narrative voice in *The Stranger*, confiding everything and somehow explaining nothing, makes for a fascinatingly repellent effect. It is not a new device. Henry James, who tried all devices, also experimented with this one; and the taciturn narrator who records surfaces but who interprets only through the set of his shoulders is the stock in trade of the American school of violence (and its European derivative), its well-worn legacy from Ernest Hemingway. But it was more probably from André Gide, and especially from his *The Immoralist*, that Camus (as Rachel Bespaloff has suggested) learned how to use the first person "to express the most intimate experience with the maximum detachment." What results is a disturbing blend of the cozy and the clammy: a blend close to the central meaning of the novel—what it is about, what it wants to bring into being. For the aim of *The Stranger* is to realize the exact sensation of absurdity. Meursault is what Camus would presently define in *The Myth of Sisyphus* as an absurd man: that is, a man whose indifference matches the indifference of the universe; a man with the instinct of the unreason in the heart of things; who has long since substituted quantity for quality in every human context; who sees, without any sense of the pain of loss, no blood relation whatever between himself and the earth he inhabits. It is Meursault's destiny, like that of many another tragic hero, to suffer toward the discovery of his own identity: to take upon himself, knowingly at the last, the burden of humanity.

Detachment, indifference, the absence of causal relations, a present unflanked by a remembered past or a hoped-for future: all of that belongs to the configuration of absurdity as a human attribute; and all of it marks the narrative style of *The Stranger*. The unremitting skill with which it does so makes Camus's first novel, in my judgment, his most successful literary achievement to date (with the possible exception of the artistically incommensurable play, *Caligula*). *The Plague* takes in more of life and has a more intrusively satisfactory moral content; but it appeals perhaps more strongly to the ethical than to the aesthetic sense.[12] There is, on the contrary, an almost exasperating perfection about the plan and the execution of *The Stranger*. It has the air of a tour de force; its magic is occasionally only the magic of the skilled illusionist. But it seems to be invulnerable: what is happening in it is happening at every instant; and its sustained sterility turns out to be surprisingly fertile—the book grows differently in different minds, but it never fails to grow.

The atmosphere that greets us at once compares tellingly with the confessional fervor of *Noces*. Here is the opening sentence of the latter, from the first essay, "Nuptials at Tipasa":

In the spring, Tipasa is inhabited by the gods, and the gods talk in the sunlight and the odor of absinthe, the sea plated with silver, the sky an unbleached blue, the ruins covered with flowers and huge bubbles of light amid the heaps of stones.

Here is the beginning of *The Stranger*:

Today my mother died. Or perhaps yesterday. I don't know. I received a telegram from the Home: "Mother deceased. Burial tomorrow. Sincere condolences." That tells me nothing. Perhaps it was yesterday.

The staccato quality of those sentences reaches through style to one of the novel's underlying principles: the degree to which things normally related—*attached* to each other—have become staccato. Here, for instance, is verbally enacted the fragmentation of time. In the absurd vision, the sense of before and after—which Kant once found embedded in the mind's structure—has vanished. There is no real yesterday as distinguished from tomorrow, and events pulsate dimly in a permanent present. Nor is there any discernible causal relation: the concept of cause no longer pushes perceptions into a usable order; Meursault's favorite conjunction is the colorless "and"— never "since," "because," or "therefore."[13] The experience he recounts emerges timelessly and inexplicably out of nothing— "by a sort of respiratory spasm," as Sartre has finely noted. It emerges, too, out of the silence that pervades the novel's opening pages: as Meursault cuts people short or does not reply; as silences last too long—"the silence of these people was telling on my nerves." . . .

And it is, of course, the unimportance and the sameness of actions that are justified in the climax by the vision of death, the dark breeze blowing in toward Meursault from the years to come, equalizing everything on its way. Death is the discovered perspective of the novel: the story's beginning, its middle, and its end. *The Stranger* opens with the death and burial of the mother, and it closes on the eve of Meursault's public execution—for a murder committed at the arithmetic center of the book. We are even given a preview of that execution, in the memory of a similar event the father had once witnessed and reported on, which had fascinated and nauseated his father. In *The Stranger*, death has not yet gathered itself into a single tidal wave of destruction, as it will do in *The Plague*. It reveals itself only at sundry times and in sundry places, and it is just the omnipresence of death that the hero must come to understand. That is the substance of his tragic perception, akin to the perception of the interplay of fate and freedom that often rounded out a Greek tragedy.

For willfully stunted though it is, and with everything said in a casual undertone, *The Stranger* does represent one of the modes of tragedy: tragedy, that is, as the critique of tragedy. The traditional rhythm of tragedy—to borrow the useful terms of Francis Fergusson[14]—moves from a *purpose* (do something about the Theban plague; revenge the killing of the former king) through a *passion* (the suffering of the hero, as conflict arises from the pursuit of his purpose) to a *perception* (the wisdom begotten of suffering). *The Stranger* is in some sense less a version of than a comment on that inherited pattern: a critique of it, almost a parody. For *The Stranger* moves from carefully realized purposelessness through a prolonged absence of passion to the perception that makes them both right and appropriate. It is, in short, the absurd mimesis of the tragic.

Notes

12. I do not mean to say, at least without discussion, that this is a bad thing for a novel to do. We must also reckon with Camus's own curious but logical theory of the literary art: that a book is a kind of thrust of the spirit under very particular circumstances; so that circumstances warranting one type of expression at one moment may require something rather different at another.

13. The only passage in the novel where causal relations are asserted is the speech for the prosecution at Meursault's trial. The presence of such relations is one reason why Meursault feels that the speech is about someone else, not about himself.

14. In *The Idea of a Theater* (Princeton, 1949). Mr. Fergusson acknowledges a partial debt to Kenneth Burke for these terms; and both Mr. Fergusson and Burke are indebted to the *Poetics* of Aristotle.

ALAIN ROBBE-GRILLET POINTS TO METAPHORS AND ANTHROPOMORPHISM

Albert Camus, as we know, has named *absurdity* the impassable gulf which exists between man and the world, between the aspirations of the human mind and the world's incapacity to satisfy them. Absurdity is in neither man nor things, but in the impossibility of establishing between them any relation other than *strangeness*.

Every reader has noticed, nonetheless, that the hero of *The Stranger* maintains an obscure complicity with the world, composed of rancor and fascination. The relations of this man with the objects surrounding him are not at all innocent: absurdity constantly involves disappointment, withdrawal, rebellion. It is no exaggeration to claim that it is things, quite specifically, which ultimately lead this man to crime: the sun, the sea, the brilliant sand, the gleaming knife, the spring among the rocks, the revolver. . . . As, of course, among these things, the leading role is taken by Nature.

Thus the book is not written in a language as *filtered* as the first pages may lead one to believe. Only, in fact, the objects already charged with a flagrant human content are carefully neutralized, and *for moral reasons* (such as the old mother's coffin, whose screws are described in terms of their shape and the depth they penetrate into the wood). Alongside this we discover, increasingly numerous as the moment of the murder approaches, the most revealing classical metaphors, naming man or infected by his omnipresence: the countryside is "swollen with sunlight," the evening is "like a melancholy truce," the rutted road reveals the "shiny flesh" of the tar, the soil is "the color of blood," the sun is a "blinding rain," its reflection on a shell is "a sword of light," the day has "cast anchor in an ocean of molten metal"—not to mention the "breathing" of the "lazy" waves, the "somnolent" headland, the sea that "pants" and the "cymbals" of the sun. . . .

The crucial scene of the novel affords the perfect image of a painful solidarity: the implacable sun is always "the same," its reflection on the blade of the knife the Arab is holding "strikes" the hero full in the face and "searches" his eyes, his hand tightens on the revolver, he tries to "shake off" the sun, he fires again, four times. "And it was—he says—as though I had knocked four times on the door of unhappiness."

Absurdity, then, is really a form of tragic humanism. It is not an observation of the separation between man and things. It is a lover's quarrel, which leads to a crime of passion. The world is accused of complicity in a murder.

When Sartre writes (in *Situations I*) that *The Stranger* "rejects anthropomorphism," he is giving us, as the quotations above show, an incomplete view of the work. Sartre has doubtless noticed these passages, but he supposes that Camus, "unfaithful to his principle, is being poetic." Can we not say, rather, that these metaphors are precisely the explanation of the book? Camus does not reject anthropomorphism, he utilizes it with economy and subtlety in order to give it more weight.

Everything is in order, since the point is ultimately, as Sartre points out, to show us, according to Pascal's phrase "the natural unhappiness of our condition."

PATRICK HENRY COMPARES THE WORK OF CAMUS AND VOLTAIRE

Coming out of an age where reason was deemed all powerful in metaphysics and psychology, Voltaire adopted the modest empirical viewpoint and wrote endlessly to indicate that reason would only be efficacious if it were linked to human experience. Camus reached the same views although he came from a heritage that had little faith left in reason.

Both Voltaire and Camus realized that reason would never fathom metaphysics or the problems of evil and human destiny. Nevertheless, they refused to have recourse to the non-material or the transcendental to solve the problem of knowledge, as did Pascal, Rousseau, Kierkegaard, Jaspers and other men they severely criticized. These thinkers had taken the leap of faith, which Voltaire and Camus could not do. For them, either reason, grounded in human experience, answered the riddle of human destiny or nothing did. And, as Camus clearly indicates, nothing did: 'La raison est vaine et il n'y a rien au-delà de la raison' (*ESS*. 124).

Due to this paradoxical metaphysical situation, Camus devised a theory of absurdity in *Le Mythe de Sisyphe* which is fictionally present in *L'Etranger*. The 'novel' contains the two levels of absurdity already present and portrayed in theoretical detail in *Le Mythe*: the metaphysical and the social. The hero, Meursault, who resembles in many ways the hero of *Le Mythe*, can be seen as the *homo absurdus* of *Le Mythe* either from the beginning of the narrative or only at its conclusion. Like the hero of *Le Mythe*, he is a stranger among men because he prefers nature to convention and in the second part of the 'novel' he becomes fully cognizant of that alienation.

Unlike the hero of *Le Mythe*, Meursault is not a stranger to the universe even though he is rationally unable to order it, for he is well adapted to the cosmos and never 'de trop' before nature. He resembles the hero of *Le Mythe* in that he is a stranger to himself and is also a stranger, to varying degrees, to the reader. He exemplifies 'everyman' precisely because of his status as outsider. . . .

Meursault goes to his death happy—'il faut imaginer Sisyphe heureux' (*ESS*. 198)—and the 'novel' ends with the recognition that the protagonist is and has been happy. All through the work the intertwining leitmotifs of absurdity and happiness have been present. . . .

Like Meursault, Candide is a stranger to other men and to himself; unlike Meursault, he is a stranger to the world. *Candide* depicts absurdity at both the social and metaphysical levels and conforms to the notion of divorce and confrontation inherent in the definition of absurdity outlined by Camus in the *Mythe de Sisyphe*. As in *L'Etranger*, we find a network of thematic and stylistic devices that enforce the impression of absurdity at both levels.

There is much critical commentary as to the precise moment that Meursault becomes aware of the absurd, whether this takes place before the narrative begins or only at the conclusion of the tale. In the case of *Candide*, there is no full consciousness of the absurd until the conclusion of the conte, for *Candide* is a Bildungsroman, 'un roman d'apprentissage'.

BRIAN T. FITCH ON INTERPRETATION AND MISINTERPRETATION

The whole of the second part of *L'Etranger* is thus centred on the problem of interpretation or more precisely that of inaccurate interpretation. All this interpretative activity is occasioned precisely by the events recounted in the first part. In other words, the second part proposes a number of interpretations or reconstitutions of the preceding part. What is important in the present context is that the reader is convinced of the inaccuracy of a given interpretation (that of the examining magistrate, Meursault's lawyer, or the prosecuting counsel, for example) *not* because it departs from any of the other interpretations proposed since all they have in common is their fictive status as *a posteriori* fabrications, but rather because of the heavy irony[18] that pervades all the scenes involving the confrontation between Meursault and the various representatives of the legal system. This irony rules out any misinterpretation by the reader of the way he is to evaluate the portraits of the protagonist that emerge during the trial and its preliminaries. However, as we shall see, this is not the only operative factor in this respect. What I wish to stress for the moment is that nowhere in the second part of the novel is there provided any explicit corrective of these false portraits of Meursault.

The next and vital stage in my argument is constituted by the recognition of the curious and unexpected similarity between the false Meursault(s) evoked by the lawyers and the person the reader of the first part had begun to see in his mind's eye before his arrest and trial. This similarity is surprising to say the least and its implications are far-reaching. But before examining them, we must first establish the accuracy of such a comparison.

That the prosecuting lawyer's description of Meursault is virtually identical to the considered interpretation of his character by many readers may be a source of surprise for any left-wing intellectual reader, but it is nonetheless true, as can be readily demonstrated by quoting certain critics, not all among the most obtuse. For example, Jean Onimus considers that Meursault 'nous provoque par son inhumanité' and is led to exclaim that if, as Céleste maintains, 'Meursault est un homme, la vie humaine est impossible.'[19] As for Pierre-Henri Simon, the kind of detachment and indifference that Meursault exhibits 'le place hors de la normale.'[20] Charles Moeller, for his part, feels that 'son absence de sens moral est effrayante' and goes so far as to claim that 'il y a du malade chez lui.'[21] In short, the character is seen by such critics as being, at best, a kind of pathological case. In fact, he can even inspire a positive hatred rather than pity, as he does for Pierre Descaves who sees him as 'une sorte de somnambule' who disgusts him: 'Personnage sommaire et somme toute assez odieux, qui ne peut que dégoûter.'[22]

Moreover, these opinions are based, it should be stressed, on a reading of the *whole* of the novel, including its second part, whereas what I am maintaining here is that the reader can well form such an opinion of the protagonist in reading the account of the events preceding the last chapter of the first part. I am not even claiming that there be any inevitability about his forming such an opinion but rather that the opportunity to do so is clearly offered by the text. These distinctions are important.

To understand how the Meursault of the events leading up to the murder can create the impression of being in some way abnormal is not difficult and it would be fastidious and indeed superfluous to go over yet again critical ground[23] that has been covered time and again. It is his apparent indifference that can be interpreted as complete insensitivity that has caused many a reader to react, in the first instance, after a moment of perplexity, with a feeling of revulsion for the protagonist. His indifference, which manifests itself as a kind of automatic reaction in his constant retort 'Cela m'était égal,' covers virtually every aspect of his existence except his corporal contact with the sand, the sea, and the sky of North Africa, or so it seems to the reader. The lack of career motivation he shows when his employer offers him the chance to go to work in Paris (cf. I, 1153–4), a traditional form of promotion in the context of the French community wherever it may be, is no doubt the least surprising. The exchange between Meursault and his mistress Marie, who seeks to determine the precise nature of his feelings for her and his consequent degree of commitment to their relationship is, however, much more disquieting to the reader and becomes more so as their conversation proceeds. Indeed, Marie's conclusion that her lover is 'bizarre' may well seem to be a rather generous evaluation of his attitude!

Notes

18. Note, for example, the rôle of the curious form of free indirect reported speech I have analysed elsewhere (cf. 'Aspects de l'emploi du discours indirect libre dans *L'Etranger*,' *Albert Camus* 1, 'Autour de *L'Etranger*' [1968] 81–91).

19. Jean Onimus, *Camus* (Paris: Desclée de Brouwer 1965) 65–6.

20. Pierre-Henri Simon, *Présence de Camus* (Paris: Nizet 1962) 48.

21. Charles Moeller, *Littérature du XXe siècle et christianisme. I. Silence de Dieu* (Tournai-Paris: Casterman 1954) 55.

22. Pierre Descaves, 'Albert Camus et le roman,' *La Table ronde* 146 (février 1960) 52–3.

23. Cf. *Narrateur et narration . . .*, 2nd ed. (1968) 27–39.

PATRICK MCCARTHY ON THE MOTHER IMAGE

The reader is also conscious that this is a French-Algerian day. Most of the elements mentioned—the values of the body, the lack of reflection, the camaraderie and the superficial sense of belonging to nature—are ingredients of pied-noir culture. It follows that the flaw in this happiness will take the form of the Arabs, whom Meursault has already described in a memorable sentence: 'They looked at us in silence but in their way, neither more nor less than if we were stones or dead trees' (79).

We are tempted to interpret this by using Sartre's concept of negritude. In colonial societies the vision of the colonizer dominates, and the colonized are obliged to look at themselves as their master does. There comes a moment, however, when the colonized assert their identity against their master by compelling him to submit to their gaze. If this interpretation is true, then Camus is building up the tension in the novel: the 'they', the Arabs, are turning against the 'us', the French-Algerians.

However we are even more struck by the way the Arab's look resembles Meursault's. If the Arab is characterized by indifference—it is here that Camus rejoins the mainstream of French-Algerian writing—then he is another Meursault. Like him, the Arab takes no account of inner life, but rather destroys the elements that are traditionally considered human. He does to Meursault what Meursault had done to the pensioners. Further parallels between the two lie in their cult of silence and their alienation from the values of work and commerce. So not merely does the Arab threaten Meursault because he is the agent of the mother and a rival claimant to the womanhood and land of Algeria, but he is also Meursault's brother, a more

64

authentic Meursault. In this respect, too, he is a menace to Meursault's identity.

After the account of the lunch, the language of the chapter changes and grows ever more lyrical. Sense impressions take on more than physical force, and a hallucination is created where Meursault is brutalized. His enemy is the sun—'its glare reflected from the sea was unbearable' (85); it is 'overwhelming' (89) and his head 'resounds with sun' (91); the light falls like 'blinding rain' (91). The other objects of nature help to create an inferno: 'heat like stone wells up from the ground' (85), while the sand is 'red-hot' (86). Even the sea betrays Meursault, for 'a dense, fiery breath rises up from it' (95).

Meanwhile time is suspended: 'For two hours the day had not advanced' (93). In the previous sentence the adjective 'same' is repeated three times. Space has shrunk to the beach on which no one is present except the three Europeans and the two Arabs. The sense of ritual is heightened by the use of adjectives like 'equal' and 'regular' (86), while a colour structure is created by the domination of red which is the colour of male sexuality and aggression.

It is more correct to talk of an inferno than of natural objects, because these pages are dominated by what Sartre calls 'word-objects'. They are clustered around the motif of disintegration: 'the sun was breaking itself into pieces on the sand' (89), while two pages later there is 'an explosion of red' (91). And the figure to be destroyed is Meursault: 'all this heat weighed on me and barred my path' (92); a page later the attack comes from the opposite direction—'an entire beach alive with sunshine pressed me from behind' (93). His existence menaced, Meursault struggles to survive: 'I strained as hard as I could to overcome the sun' (92). The metaphor of the sunlight as a sword-blade is invoked to heighten the danger. As in Chapter 1, but more clearly so, Meursault is near to death.

We are able to link the sun with the Arab in his complementary roles as agent of the mother and enemy of the pied-noir. Each time Meursault goes to the beach, it is to avoid remaining with the women. The first time the reason is the male–female division of labour, where the women remain to wash the dishes. Although the second case is less clear, Meursault's willingness to accompany Raymond may be explained by his dislike of the emotion the women show at Raymond's wound—'Madame Masson was crying and Marie was very pale' (88). This reminds us of Meursault's refusal to weep at his mother's funeral and also of his refusal to intervene, as Marie asks him to do, when Raymond beats up the Arab woman. So his decision to accompany Raymond marks a rejection of woman in her role as creature of tenderness.

When Meursault returns to the beach for the third time, it is in order not to 'approach the women once more' (91), and later he adds that he is seeking shade to 'flee from the sun, struggle and women's tears' (92). This juxtaposition sums up Meursault's dilemma. If the sun be accepted as an image of the mother, then Meursault is fleeing both the indifferent mother and the tender Marie. He is still unable to free himself from the former by caring for the latter.

But the mother accompanies him to the beach: the colour white is present in the sea-shells which throw back the sun and the colour black in the boat that is out at sea. Moreover, the comparison with the funeral is made via the key adjective 'same': 'It was the same sun as the day when I had buried mother.' Jean Gassin is correct in viewing Meursault's attack on the Arab as a gesture against the mother who is bringing him close to death.

JOHN FLETCHER EXPLAINS CAMUS'S MANIPULATION OF THE READER

In any case, what could be more characteristic of the *nouveau roman* than Camus's handling of Meursault's rhetoric in *L'Etranger*? The cunning with which Meursault manipulates the reader and alienates his/her sympathies away from the murdered Arab is the invention of a writer who was fully aware that reality is created by language—a premise of the *nouveau roman*—rather than being straightforwardly conveyed by it, as Balzac (or the Balzac whom Robbe-Grillet sets up as Aunt

Sally in *Pour un nouveau roman*) assumed. A close reading of *L'Etranger* shows how Meursault, by a cunning use of tenses and of other rhetorical devices, *creates* the version of events which virtually every reader accepts and retains: that the Arab's death was at worst a regrettable incidence of manslaughter and at best a legitimate action, on Meursault's part, in self-defence, rather than, as the prosecution allege at Meursault's trial, murder in the first degree.

That close reading has to begin at the first word, *aujourd'hui* ('Today Maman died'). Although this word is at once qualified by the words 'or yesterday maybe', the text creates a feeling of *present* time which continues throughout the first two paragraphs. For convenience, I shall refer to this feeling as the 'dramatic present', even where it is not necessarily aroused by a preponderant use of the present tense proper but by other parts of speech (such as temporal adverbs like 'today').

The third paragraph opens with a *passé composé* ('J'ai pris l'autobus à deux heures', ('*I took the two o'clock bus*'), p. 1125).[2] This constitutes one of the most important time-shifts in the whole novel, but because the *passé composé* is ambiguous in French—it can apply to a very recent occurrence, and usually does, but (particularly in colloquial usage) it can also refer to the remote past—the reader is not at once aware that the narrator Meursault is gliding from an ostensible stance 'on top of events' in the first two paragraphs to a position considerably more removed in time. How far removed, the reader has no way of telling: the *passé composé* would be used by a speaker quite naturally to relate even remote occurrences, and it is this informal mode which characterises Meursault's style. Indeed, in abandoning the traditional *passé simple* (preterite) tense in favour of the more colloquial *passé composé* (perfect) tense, Camus broke new ground in French narrative prose. The reason which is usually given for this is that he wanted to give Meursault's account a conversational immediacy which would make his hero more *sympathique* (likeable) to the reader, and undoubtedly it helps in that regard. But a more important reason was the temporal ambiguity of the *passé composé*. Indeed, the first two paragraphs of the novel are fraught with ambiguity, even deceit, on the question of when the story was composed: the use of the future tense in particular ('Je prendrai l'autobus à deux heures . . . je rentrerai demain soir' ('*I'll catch the two o'clock bus . . . I'll return tomorrow evening*', p. 1125) artificially but very effectively appears to situate the narration between the mother's death and her funeral.

With the third paragraph of the novel, however, we are withdrawn imperceptibly into a structure of less immediate, more distanced narrative. The use of the preterite tense would have made this break crudely evident. The *passé composé* allows a smooth and virtually unnoticed shift. It is some while, in fact, before the reader becomes aware that Meursault is not, temporally speaking, on top of the events he is describing; by using a shrewd blend of the dramatic present and the ambiguous past, Meursault is able to create an illusion both of immediacy and of objective veracity.

In fact, it is not until the fifth chapter of Part 1 that we are given some 'back perspective' on Meursault's existence *prior to* the main events of the novel, when he tells us how he had been ambitious as a student and informs Marie that he had once lived in Paris. By this point he is preparing the reader for the revelation that he is far more aware of the implications of his actions—hitherto presented as spontaneous and unconsidered, with one event simply following upon another—than, for rhetorical reasons, he has been willing to do up till now. The revelation comes on p. 1157: 'J'ai répondu', he begins, and then adds as if in parentheses, 'je ne sais pas encore pourquoi' ('*I answered, I still don't know why*'). Those last few words—je ne sais pas encore pourquoi—lift the narrative clear out of ambiguous time and situate it firmly in the unambiguous remote past, since they refer to the 'real' present, and betray the fact that the account is being written with the benefit of considerable hindsight.

How much hindsight, the reader must still wait to discover, but in due course, by a process of elimination, he/she establishes that the book, which at the outset appears to be a diary, is in fact *entirely* composed, from beginning to end, in the days (or hours) which follow the rejection of the prisoner's appeal and the consequential certitude it brings that the time he has left is finite. How then does Meursault spend the precious hours (or days) before his execution? On something which, unlike his naive student aspirations, he has at last found to possess 'real importance': nothing less than conducting his defence all over again, not the assize court affair which resulted in his conviction for first degree murder, but the trial he pleads before us, the jury composed of his posthumous readers. For it is *our* favourable verdict that he is after, and our sympathy which is of supreme importance to him. He is thus a more self-aware and sophisticated narrator—and indeed a more consistent character—than is usually supposed. He is, in fact, a writer, constructing a text and therefore—Robbe-Grillet has taught us—a *reality* which *his* text calls into being.

Notes

2. *Théâtre, récits, nouvelles* (Paris: Gallimard, Bibliothèque de la Pléïade, 1963). Future references are to this edition.

JACK MURRAY ON THE NOVEL'S APPARENT COHERENCE

Le sens du livre tient exactement dans le parallélisme des deux parties. (*Carnets II*, 30)

On the formal level, the novel, in its very nature, tends toward sprawl, unconnectedness, and even anarchy, and it must therefore transcend such perils if it is to achieve the closure dictated by the canons of classicism or realism. Closure is not simply a formal matter, but because of the necessary logical connectedness that it imposes on all the narrative content of any particular work, it becomes an ideological matter as well. Its principal danger is that it may impose a monological construal or reading of the events recounted, whereas a move away from closure would advance into chaos where no coherent reading would be possible at all. Few works in the modern period illustrate both the formal and ideological dimensions of the problem at issue here better than Albert Camus's *L'Étranger*. While firmly installed within both the realist and classical traditions, the novel nonetheless enacts an extensive debate between two contending sides over closure, underscoring the contention by an elaborate displacement process that must be designated as allegory. Because the crucial matter of the murder dictates that the dialectic set up between either side inevitably becomes trapped in its own illogic, the reader who endeavors to interpret the text finds himself in the position of the author's Sisyphus: just at the point when he feels that he is approaching some final construal, he must begin the whole interpretive task over again.

At first sight, the work appears totally coherent and harmonious and recalls the compact economy of a Gidean *récit*.[1] Because of this, the seeming randomness and disjointedness of the first part are only a calculated literary illusion. Moreover, its scattered parts quickly join together in a whole after the arrest and during the trial, for it is then that the purpose of their narration becomes clear (see Van den Heuvel 69; Banks 15).[2] On an even more formal level, the text is divided into two fairly even halves with a blank page marked "II" dividing them. Castex demonstrates that the first five of the six chapters of the first part are answered by the five chapters of the second part, the extra sixth chapter actually being a pivot between the two sections (103).[3] Furthermore, the complete antithesis in character of the two parts, if anything, only enhances their clear interconnectedness in a thematic closure (if not a narrative one). Uri Eisenzweig, for example, qualifies the world described in the first five chapters as "Paradise," relativized thus by the irruption of Time after the fatal shot fired in the pivotal chapter six, which converts what has preceded into radical anteriority. The second part becomes that of the Law (of the Father), but a continual mirroring process assures a symmetrical relationship with the first part (71–75 and passim). Carl Viggiani specifies the nature of this relationship when he sees in the second section an ironic recapitulation of everything that has happened in the first part (885).

70

In this study I shall modify Viggiani's statement by proposing, instead, two contending construals of the same series of narrative elements, Meursault's and the prosecutor's. If the murder is not in doubt, there is a considerable difference of opinion between the two figures over the relevance to it of a series of episodes preceding it: the protagonist's behavior at the mother's funeral and his actions in the days following. Meursault sees no connection whatsoever, whereas the prosecutor most emphatically does (see McCarthy 68). In the latter instance, one may say that the prosecutor imposes radical narrative closure on the elements over against Meursault's position (the "anticlosure" one) that they are unrelated, adventitious, and inconsequential—a position, in short, that leans toward narrative "anarchy."[4] If one adheres to the standard narratological line that the *histoire* or *fable* must consist of a string of events in which each constitutes a transformation that leads causally to the next (Prince 17–18), then only Meursault's involvement with Raymond, the altercation with the Arabs, and the murder itself (with the consequent imprisonment, trial, and death sentence) are connected.[5] By contrast, if one believes that character produces destiny, then recounting episodes in which the protagonist's character is revealed through his behavior has some relevance to the final outcome (see Rimmon-Kenan 35). Necessarily, a disagreement on these issues has ideological overtones that transcend the purely formal. . . .

When we take up Meursault's version of what happened,[8] we see that, while it follows the conventional chronological pattern already mentioned, it does so in an often artfully haphazard way.[9] This is but the beginning of the move toward anticlosure. For example, Meursault's account contains many elements that are extraneous to the events leading up to the murder, elements that pertain to the ordinary routines of his everyday life, to background material, etc. The latter have the effect of making the strictly narrative elements (i.e., those events that really do lead up to the murder) appear more relative in importance, if not actually devalued, so that they seem not to be the strongly marked (and transformational) events customary in closely structured narrative. The description of, and insistence on, routine, in particular, produces such an effect. The dominant perspective of routine means that unusual events such as the mother's death become only interruptions in the mechanical repetition of Meursault's life and either constitute unsettling intrusions or else do not have any clear importance at all at the time of their occurrence. In general, all this is consonant with a narrator who suffers events as they come along.

Notes

1. While pointing out this parallel, Gerald V. Banks also insists on the differences between Camus's handling of the form and Gide's (13–14). In this article I shall hold to the working premise that *L'Étranger* is a *novel*, although it is only right to point out that there has been much debate about its exact genre, let alone its proper conformity to the genre chosen (see Barrier 16).

2. Pierre-Georges Castex, who uses the author approach to the novel, suggests a tantalizing course that the genesis of the novel may have taken—namely, Camus's having to link together three quite disparate and plainly unrelated bits of narrative: a character condemned to die who refuses all consolation; a mother's funeral; a tough man and his fight with his mistress's brother (17–26). From this angle, Camus may well have found himself in the typical creative dilemma faced by any writer who must assemble a coherent and unified body out of such *disjecta membra*—in other words, attain closure. Alain Costes looks on the fragments as literary versions of obsessive phantasms that occur throughout Camus's earliest writings (57–62).

3. Brian T. Fitch stresses the stylistic difference between chapter six and the chapters that have gone before, particularly the intrusion of highly metaphorical language (42–44).

4. The formal issue is also construed by some commentators in the framework of parataxis versus syntaxis, Meursault's account being highly paratactic. See Goldschläger and Lemaire, 186. As for the ideological side, Sartre laid down the opposition between the two construals as "*le flux quotidien et amorphe de la réalité vécue*" against "*la recomposition édifiante de cette réalité par la raison humaine et le discours*." The reader will consider the flux so convincing that he will be unable to recognize it in its transposed form at the trial where it has been fed through prefabricated verbal structures (110–11).

5. Gerald V. Banks divides the sequence involving Raymond into eight stages, each one of which accelerates and increases Meursault's active involvement in his neighbor's plot (49).

6. Eisenzweig puts this the other way around: the falsity of the prosecutor's account, to the extent that it has a specular relationship with

the other account (i.e., as a form of *mise-en-abyme*), necessarily reflects on the status of the first one—makes it "true" (7). Oddly, such a perception of Meursault does little to make him more sympathetic to the reader: he tends to remain too much an unknown quantity (see Fitch 36).

7. This detail has been noted by many critics. Sartre himself pointed out the secret humor of the novel and suggested similarities with the *conte philosophique* (116). See also Banks 55; Barrier 69–70, McCarthy 71. Fitch develops Sartre's suggestion even further, seeing in Meursault's focalization of the trial a calculated and Candide-like innocence that transforms the whole judicial procedure into a satire on social structures (60, 62–64).

8. A considerable amount of ingenious discussion has endeavored to cast his version (which takes up the first part of the novel) as a *journal intime*. Such an interpretation has had to concentrate on the play of temporal references and verb tenses in the individual chapters, because there are no conventional textual markers indicating the form (e.g., dates at the head of each textual division, etc.). I agree with Maurice-Georges Barrier (27–28) that such efforts are useless and that we are dealing with a stylistic or mere literary procedure enabling the reader to experience the events of Meursault's life as he lives them. Patrick McCarthy, of course, finds an unexpected lode, when he suggests that Meursault's account, to the extent that it borrows from the *journal intime*, parodies, and thereby criticizes, the form itself, one highly favored by other authors who had gone before Camus at the prestigious house of Gallimard, publisher of *L'Étranger* (26, 99).

9. Renée Balibar, for example, cites the temporal incoherence of the third paragraph of the first chapter of the novel (113). To this must be added Barrier's notation of the way each of the first five chapters begins in the morning with awakening or with Meursault at work, and ends with evening (92).

AVI SAGI ON THE NOVEL'S REAL CONCERN: SOCIAL ALIENATION

The basic premise of this book, as noted, is that Camus's thought is a contest with the meaning of existence. In *The Myth of Sisyphus*, Camus provides one answer to this question, but his explication of existence is dynamic. To understand the innovation entailed in Camus's view of the absurd, I devote a special discussion to *The Outsider*, which appeared several months before *The Myth of Sisyphus*.

The narrative framework of *The Outsider* is straightforward: Meursault, the protagonist, is a clerk who receives a message informing him of his mother's death in an old-aged home. He travels to her funeral and, after his return, goes out with his friend Raymond. Raymond becomes entangled in a squabble with a group of Arabs and, in the course of it, Meursault shoots one of the Arabs to death. Thus ends Part I of the story. Part II is Meursault's trial, in which he will not only answer the charge of the Arab's killing, but also of the moral killing of his mother. Meursault is sentenced to death, and in his prison cell conducts several conversations with the priest, who tries to lead him to faith. He rejects this option, and persists to the end in his commitment to immanent existence, even when facing the threat of death.

Yet, beyond this narrative framework, the story is strange and remains, in a way, a dark, unsolved riddle. We think we are reading this account in Meursault's journal, but is Meursault the narrator? On the surface, the story traces the course of events in a kind of present continuous, as set by the opening line: "Mother died today. Or, maybe, yesterday; I can't be sure." This style, however, leads to an interesting paradox. In Part 1, Meursault emerges as a man whose being is constituted by immediate experience; he is not a reflective creature reexamining his existence. Meursault even says so himself. When his lawyer asks him if he had been grieved by his mother's death, "I answered that in recent years I'd rather lost the habit of noting my feelings, and hardly knew what to answer" (*The Outsider*, pp. 68–69).

Meursault's statement about himself is ambivalent, since his very description as unreflective is a reflective statement. The wording of this declaration hints to a past in which reflection had been present and, although now intentionally forsaken, is still considered a real option. Were Meursault an unreflective creature deeply engulfed in his immediate experience, he would not have kept a journal and would not have reported the experience, since these actions transcend immediacy. The narrator must therefore be, in Robert C. Solomon's formulation, "another Meursault, a reflective Meursault... It is this second Meursault who is the narrator" (Solomon, 1987, p. 250). But this Meursault is not the one of the story since, as noted, the story is written in the present continuous. Solomon therefore concludes: "Meursault of part I is an impossible character because he is both the reflective transcendental narrator and the unreflective bearer of experience" (*ibid*. See also Sprintzen, 1988, p. 25).

This genre, where the "self" is hero and narrator at the same time is common in French literature, and André Gide also resorts to it. Patrick McCarthy describes this genre, which endows inner life with a unique significance:

> The reader becomes a confidant who is seduced into believing what the "I" reveals, while the character usually develops throughout the book; by the time he becomes a narrator at the end, he can look back and trace his evolution. So there is a series of presuppositions: that the inner life is important and can be discussed with someone else, and that it is coherent. (McCarthy 1988, p. 26)

Camus's use of this genre is puzzling because Meursault, at least in Part I, rejects these approaches: "Camus has selected the literary form that requires the highest degree of awareness and has inserted into it a narrator whose very identity consists in the inadequacy of his awareness" (*ibid*.). According to McCarthy, this is Camus's innovation: using the genre in order to challenge it. He thereby seeks to demonstrate that harmony in a work of art is illusory (*ibid*., p. 25). . . .

Camus rejects Jean-Paul Sartre's view of literary writing as an outlet for the absurd, because this approach ascribes to literature a power it lacks: to provide the experience of existence. In *The Outsider*, to some extent a self-negating work, Camus offers a new artistic formulation of this idea. This move is not surprising, since, for Camus, as for Søren Kierkegaard (Sagi, 2000), the contest with existence must unfold in life and not in writing. We require, therefore, a literary form that challenges its own existence. Sartre senses this when he states that *"The Stranger* is not an explanatory book" (Sartre, 1962, p. 111), and McCarthy adds: "it *ostentatiously* does not explain" (McCarthy 1988, p. 30, emphasis in original). For Camus, "art is no different from the rest of the universe and should not pretend to a harmony or a perfection which it cannot possess" (*ibid.*, p. 31). This enigmatic novel views existence as a riddle, and conveys this in its literary design. . . .

In his interpretation of *The Outsider*, Camus focuses on the key element in the story. Meursault faces the social world as a stranger, failing to share its values because he is honest with himself. He is not willing to participate in the mourning over his mother and share in her friends' solidarity because he feels nothing toward her. Meursault's loyalty to himself leads to his rift with society.

Camus points out that this self-honesty is the negative expression of the passion for truth. Instead of just a refusal, the negation expresses a passion for the absolute. Meursault, like Christ, is ready to die on the altar of this truth.

This distinctively social perspective, and not the experience of the absurd, is the deep meaning of the story. Meursault is estranged from society, and this work in no way hints to metaphysical concepts of the absurd in the style of *The Myth of Sisyphus*.

Works Cited

Camus, Albert (1961). *The Outsider*. Tr. Stuart Gilbert. Harmondsworth, England: Penguin Books.

McCarthy, Patrick, (1988). *Albert Camus: The Stranger*. Cambridge: Cambridge University Press.

Sagi, Avi (2000). *Kierkegaard, Religion, and Existence: The Voyage of the Self*, tr. Batya Stein. Amsterdam and Atlanta, Ga.: Rodopi.

Sartre, Jean-Paul. (1962). "An Explication of *The Stranger*." In *A Collection of Critical Essays*, ed. Germaine Brée. Englewood Cliffs, N.J.: Prentice Hall.

Solomon, Robert C. (1987). *From Hegel to Existentialism*. New York: Oxford University Press.

Sprintzen, David (1988). *Camus: A Critical Examination*. Philadelphia: Temple University Press.

The lie—it lies at the very heart of French existentialism. It is the infamy of the human condition for Sartre, the gravest sin for Camus. But where Sartre suspects that the lie—or what he calls *mauvaise foi*—is inescapable, Camus glorifies his characters—and apparently himself—as men without a lie. Meursault, Camus tells us in a retrospective interpretation, "refuses to lie . . . accepts death for the sake of truth."[2] Dr. Rieux of *The Plague* refuses to release information to Tarrou the reporter unless Tarrou reports "without qualification," and Rieux himself insists on taking an absurdly "objective" stance toward the plague and his reporting. Clamence of *The Fall* has been living a lie, so he is now in Purgatory (the seedy inner circles of Amsterdam), a judge-penitent: a judge, we come to see, of other people's hidden falsehoods, a penitent for his own past lie of a life. In *The Myth of Sisyphus*, it is "the absurd" that becomes the ascertainable truth, and it is the absurd hero who "keeps the absurd alive" with his defiant recognition of that truth. (By contrast, "philosophical suicide" is, in effect, a lie to oneself about the ultimate absurdity of life.) In the turmoil of French leftist politics through the Algerian crises and the Stalin show trials, Camus portrays himself in his *Notebooks* and in *The Rebel* as the "independent intellectual," the spokesman for the truth who refuses to accept the necessary political fabrications of the Left during a time of crisis and change. Accordingly, Camus has himself been interpreted and praised as the hero and martyr for the truth, as "Saint Just," the absurd hero and existential champion of honesty.

The Stranger is the best known of Camus' works, and it is on the basis of this early short novel that the interpretations of Camus' philosophy reasonably begin. (Its predecessor, *A Happy Death*, is generally considered a "test run." It was virtually "stillborn" until it was resurrected after years of *The Stranger's* success.[3]) But virtually every interpretation of *The Stranger* has culminated in what I want to argue is a false claim—that

Meursault is a totally honest man, the "stranger" who does not lie. In his own retrospective interpretation of *The Stranger*, Camus writes:

> The hero of the book is condemned because he doesn't play the game. In this sense he is a stranger to the society in which he lives; he drifts in the margin, in the suburb of private, solitary, sensual life. This is why some readers are tempted to consider him as a waif. You will have a more precise idea of this character, or one at all events in closer conformity with the intentions of the author, if you ask yourself in what way Meursault doesn't play the game. The answer is simple: He refuses to lie. Lying is not only saying what is not true. It is also and especially saying more than is true and, as far as the human heart is concerned, saying more than one feels. This is what we all do every day to simplify life. Meursault, despite appearances, does not wish to simplify life. He says what is true. He refuses to disguise his feelings and immediately society feels threatened. He is asked, for example, to say that he regrets his crime according to the ritual formula. He replies that he feels about it more annoyance than real regret and this shade of meaning condemns him.
>
> Meursault for me is then not a waif, but a man who is poor and naked, in love with the sun which leaves no shadows. Far from it being true that he lacks all sensibility, a deep tenacious passion animates him, a passion for the absolute and for truth. It is a still negative truth, the truth of being and of feeling, but one without which no victory over oneself and over the world will ever be possible. You would not be far wrong then in reading *The Stranger* as a story of a man who, without any heroics, accepts death for the sake of truth. I have some times said, and always paradoxically, that I have tried to portray in this character the only Christ we deserved. You will understand after these explanations that I said this without any intention of blasphemy and only with the slightly ironic affection which an artist has the right to feel towards the characters whom he has created.[4]

And throughout the standard interpretations, the same theme is routinely repeated, for example, "This indifferent man is intractable in his absolute respect for truth," and "His principal characteristic appears to be a kind of total sincerity which disconcerts us because it is virtually unknown in our world."[5]

This view has been challenged, but only in its scope, not in its essence. Notably, Conor Cruise O'Brien, in his *Camus*, argued that the "Meursault of the actual novel is not quite the same person as the Meursault of the commentaries. Meursault in the novel lies. He concocts for Raymond the letter that is designed to deceive the Arab girl and expose her to humiliation, and later he lies to the police to get Raymond discharged, . . . It is simply not true that Meursault is 'intractable in his absolute respect for the truth.' These episodes show him as indifferent to truth as he is to cruelty."[6] O'Brien continues to point out that Meursault, as the mirror of his author, is also indifferent to the reality of the hostility of the Arabs, the political tensions and sufferings of the Arab population, and the pretensions and arrogance of colonialism in which he plays an undisputed, even if unwitting, part. Perhaps O'Brien does not make enough of the distinction between lying and being simply indifferent to the truth, saying less than is true. In the passages in question, it is more indifference at stake than outright lying. For example, Meursault passes no judgment on Raymond's action apart from a banal appraisal of his means to an end: "I agreed it wasn't a bad plan—it would punish her all right" (40). And there is nothing in the description of the letter or his testimony before the police to make us certain that he has lied. But Camus, again in his commentary, explicitly points out that lying is not just saying what is not true. It is "also saying more than is true" and, we may safely extrapolate, saying less than is true as well. On this basis, we ought to agree with O'Brien that Meursault is, even if he does not lie outright, less than the ideal honest man. But ultimately, even O'Brien joins in the standard interpretation, qualifying it beyond the usual blanket judgment. . . .

But I want to argue that this standard interpretation in all its forms is unconvincing, not just in detail but in essence, and in spite of the seemingly authoritative fact that the author has endorsed it himself. The whole question of Meursault's "honesty" and the truth about his feelings should be replaced by an examination of the presuppositions of honesty and a very different kind of thinking about "feelings." For I want to argue that the character of Meursault is not to be located in the reflective realm of truth and falsity but exclusively in the prereflective realm of simple "seeing," "feeling," and "lived experience." On the basis of the phenomenological theories that circulated around Paris in the 1940s and with which Camus was surely familiar, I want to argue that Meursault neither lies nor tells the truth, because he never reaches that (meta-) level of consciousness where truth and falsity can be articulated. Moreover, he does not even have the feelings, much less feelings about his feelings, to which he is supposed to be so true.

Notes

2. Hayden Carruth, "Introduction," in Jean-Paul Sartre, *Nausea* (New York: New Directions, 1964), vii.

3. This is actually rather confusing. Sisyphus (according to one tradition), snatched death away from the gods and thus rendered all men immortal. He was thwarted in this attempt, obviously, and in punishment for his crime he was condemned. So, in a sense, Sisyphus was already dead. He carried out his punishment in the afterlife, in what we would consider Hell. But in Hell, he is immortal, in the sense that he will never die and his punishment will never cease.

4. An excellent meditation on the agony of living forever is Bernard Williams's now classic essay, "The Makropulos Case: Reflections on the Tedium of Immortality," in his *Problems of the Self: Philosophical Papers 1956–1972* (Cambridge: Cambridge University Press, 1973), 82–100.

5. Morris Raphael Cohen, *Preface to Logic* (New York: Meridian Books, 1956.

6. Thus Heidegger, following Kierkegaard, sharply distinguishes those "syllogisms" that merely give us the impersonal conclusion that we are going to die from the profound realization, "Being-unto-Death," that we are indeed going to die. The difference here, one might argue, is also the difference between sound argument and objective truth versus the intense subjectivity of the actual experience of confronting death.

Works by Albert Camus

L'Envers et l'endroit (*The Wrong Side and the Right Side*), 1937

Noces (*Nuptials*), 1937

Le Mythe de Sisyphe: Essai sur l'absurde (*The Myth of Sisyphus and Other Essays*), 1942

L'Étranger (*The Stranger;* also published as *The Outsider*), 1942

Caligula, 1944

Le Malentendu (*The Misunderstanding;* also translated as *Cross Purpose*), 1944

La Peste (*The Plague*), 1947

L'Etat de siège (*The State of Siege*), 1948

Les Justes (*The Just Assassins*), 1949

L'Homme révolté (*The Rebel*), 1951

L'Eté (*Resistance, Rebellion, and Death*), 1954

La Chute (*The Fall*), 1956

Requiem pour une nonne (adaptor; from the novel *Requiem for a Nun* by William Faulkner), 1956

L'Exil et le royaume (*Exile and the Kingdom*), 1957

Caligula and Three Other Plays (contains *Caligula, Le Malentendu, L'Etat de Siège,* and *Les Justes*), 1958

Les Possédés (adaptor; from the novel *The Possessed* by Fydor Dostoyevsky), 1959

Lyrical and Critical Essays (includes *L'Envers et l'endroit* and *Noces*), 1967

La Mort heureuse (*A Happy Death*), 1971

Le Premier Homme (*The First Man*) unfinished novel, 1994

Annotated Bibliography

Banks, G.V. *Camus: L'Etranger*, 1976.

Banks looks at Camus's narrative technique in *The Stranger* and sees the author as using French classical form to clarify Meursault's absurdist experience. In Banks's second section, the author looks at Meursault and argues that Camus's patterns and themes show how who Meursault is has a "direct bearing" on the events that bring about the Arab's murder. In Banks's third section, he focuses on the second part of the novel and how Meursault reacts to the people in that part.

Brée, Germaine. "Heroes of Our Time: *The Stranger*." In *Camus*, 1959.

Brée sees Meursault as someone who is sacrificed and returned to the cosmos. Brée feels Meursault's earlier self was incapable of managing even a simple life. From this position of inadequacy and indifference, Meursault moves to a new place where his fatal error is that he doesn't question the meaning of life. Instead he embraces violence and death.

Bronner, Stephen Eric. "Meursault." In *Camus: Portrait of a Moralist*, 1999.

Bronner shows Meursault's life as meaningless and directionless. Meursault is condemned to death because he does not have an adequate explanation for killing the Arab. He is a stranger to himself and to the society that does not understand him. The killing lacks purpose and mirrors the meaningless world. Existence is absurd because there is "an irresolvable paradox" between an action and the subjective motivation behind it.

Brosman, Catherine Savage. *Albert Camus*. Literary Masters series, vol. 8, 2001.

This text provides a chronology, a look at Camus's life, a discussion of how Camus became a writer, and a description of what was occurring from a historical standpoint during Camus's writing life—the 1930s, World War II and the occupation, the postwar period, and the Algerian War. The work covers his writings and how they were received during different times. One section includes Camus's commentary about himself and his writing.

Favre, Frantz. "*L'Etranger* and "Metahphysical Anxiety,'" translated by Adele King. In *Camus's* L'Etranger: *Fifty Years On*, edited by Adele King, 1992.

Favre looks at *The Stranger* to see how the text has been influenced by the writings of Friedrich Nietzsche. He looks at how Nietzsche and Camus respond to metaphysics and examines Meursault in terms of Nietzsche's ideas. Favre writes of Meursault's belief that he has lived the right way and Meursault's perspective on language, for example.

Girard, René. "Camus's Stranger Retried." In *"To Double Business Bound": Essays on Literature, Mimesis, and Anthropology*, 1978.

Girard writes of the immature behavior of Meursault, who, like an undeveloped child, believes he wants to be separate from society but then realizes he is mistaken and looks for a way to gain attention. The protagonist becomes involved with a shady character. No matter what, though, the reader is to see "the hero" as innocent and the justices as unfair.

Knapp, Bettina L., ed. *Critical essays on Albert Camus*, 1988.

This text contains fourteen essays that cover key works of Camus as well as ideas his works inspire. Authors look at Camus in terms of libertarian socialism, North Africa, exile, and ethics, for example. The title ends with a tribute to Camus by Jean-Paul Sartre.

Manly, William M. "Journey to Consciousness: The Symbolic Pattern of Camus's *L'Etranger*," *PMLA* 79, no. 3 (June 1964).

Manly connects *The Stranger* to ideas in *The Myth of Sisyphus*. Specifically, he cites how Meursault develops, reaching an awakening or new consciousness that follows the themes and images of *Sisyphus*. In the end, Meursault decides to define himself by his fate at the hands of an irrational community.

Maus, Derek C. *Readings on* The Stranger, 2001.

> This compilation gives an account of Camus's life as well as an explanation of characters in the novel and its plot. Each of four sections has essays about a particular topic: philosophical themes, technical and historical aspects of the novel, works by other authors that invite comparison to the novel, and Meursault's role in causing his problems. A chronology is also included, as well as a listing of other helpful books to consult.

Onimus, Jean. *Albert Camus and Christianity*, translated by Emmett Parker, 1965.

> Onimus writes of Camus as engaging because he admits his uncertainties about life and is frank in his explanations. He says Camus "lived the 'heart of the matter'" by focusing on the essential and being simple and candid. Onimus questions whether Camus is successful in his "courageous effort" to present a new wisdom, one without God and with some grappling of the irrational.

Schofer, Peter. "The Rhetoric of the Text: Causality, Metaphor, and Irony." In *Camus's* L'Etranger: *Fifty Years on*, edited by Adele King, 1992.

> Schofer writes of the metaphors Camus uses in the text and explains the logic behind how the same metaphors are used at different points in the narration, sun and darkness being key at Meursault's mother's funeral and the murder scene, for instance. In Schofer's view, metaphor brings meaning. He also comments on questions left unanswered in the text and on Meursault's finding life through writing.

Shattuck, Roger. "Two Inside Narratives: *Billy Budd* and L'Etranger," *Texas Studies in Literature and Language* 4, no. 3 (Autumn 1962).

> Shattuck compares Melville's Billy Budd to Camus's Meursault. In the narratives that feature each of the two characters, a crime is related as an innocent action. Neither man fights the charges against him, and neither shows remorse. Shattuck points out the men's weaknesses and how this affects the way others assess them. Unlike Billy, Meursault changes.

Sprintzen, David. *"The Stranger."* In *Camus: A Critical Examination*, 1988.

Sprintzen explains why readers have an uncomfortable reaction to Meursault. In Sprintzen's view, the reader wants to identify with, and even feel sorry, for the character yet has difficulty doing so since Meursault seems so lacking in the usual emotions and aspirations of humanity. Sprintzen also draws parallels between Meursault's life and Camus's and writes of Meursault's transformation and recognition that the life he lived, and that included a rejection of society's ways, was good.

Thody, Philip. "Camus's 'L'Etranger' Revisited," *Critical Quarterly*, vol. 21, no. 2 (Summer 1979).

Thody revisits *The Stranger* with an eye toward whether the book is or is not racist. He points out how critics viewing the work were concerned with different aspects of it. Initially critics were preoccupied by the novel's absurdity, later on shifting their focus to the presence of prejudice in the text, each time filtering their responses through events of their own times that caused a heightened awareness of the particular issues and themes. Thody also looks at remarks Camus made about the book and how the author's comments fit in with the impression the book leaves on readers.

Van Den Hoven, Adrian. "Sartre's Conception of Historiality and Temporality: The Quest for a Motive in Camus' *The Stranger* and Sartre's *Dirty Hands*." *Sartre Studies International* 11 (June–December 2005).

The author compares the two works, pointing out that in books about murder the mystery usually centers on revealing the murderer's identity, whereas in these works the tension revolves around the question of why the murders were committed. Both works are also narrated in the first person, giving the reader a single perspective. Van Den Hoven considers this in light of Sartre's theoretical writings of the late 1930s. He also points out that both Sartre and Camus are intent on "the individual's right to his own view of events."

 Contributors

Harold Bloom is Sterling Professor of the Humanities at Yale University. He is the author of 30 books, including *Shelley's Mythmaking*, *The Visionary Company*, *Blake's Apocalypse*, *Yeats*, *A Map of Misreading*, *Kabbalah and Criticism*, *Agon: Toward a Theory of Revisionism*, *The American Religion*, *The Western Canon*, and *Omens of Millennium: The Gnosis of Angels, Dreams, and Resurrection*. *The Anxiety of Influence* sets forth Professor Bloom's provocative theory of the literary relationships between the great writers and their predecessors. His most recent books include *Shakespeare: The Invention of the Human*, a 1998 National Book Award finalist, *How to Read and Why*, *Genius: A Mosaic of One Hundred Exemplary Creative Minds*, *Hamlet: Poem Unlimited*, *Where Shall Wisdom Be Found?*, and *Jesus and Yahweh: The Names Divine*. In 1999, Professor Bloom received the prestigious American Academy of Arts and Letters Gold Medal for Criticism. He has also received the International Prize of Catalonia, the Alfonso Reyes Prize of Mexico, and the Hans Christian Andersen Bicentennial Prize of Denmark.

Jean-Paul Sartre was a French existentialist philosopher, novelist, playwright, and critic. He was awarded the Nobel Prize for Literature in 1964 but declined it, on the grounds that he always refused official honors and did not want to be associated with a particular institution. His best-known works include the novel *La Nausée* (*Nausea*), the philosophical publication *L'Être et le néant* (*Being and Nothingness*), and the dramas *Les Mouches* (*The Flies*) and *Huit clos* (*No Exit*).

R.W.B. Lewis is a professor emeritus of Yale. He authored *The American Adam* and several other titles.

Alain Robbe-Grillet is a leading theoretician of the "new novel." He authored *Les Gommes* (*The Erasers*), *Le Voyeur* (*The Voyeur*), and other titles and is also a filmmaker.

Patrick Henry is Cushing Eells Professor Emeritus of Philosophy and Literature at Whitman College in Walla Walla, Washington. He is the author most recently of *We Only Know Men: The Rescue of Jews in France during the Holocaust*.

Brian T. Fitch has taught at Trinity College and the University of Toronto. He has authored work on Camus and written other texts as well, including *Beckett and Babel*.

Patrick McCarthy is chair of the English department at the University of Miami. Among other titles, he has written *Camus* and *Ulysses: Portals of Discovery*.

John Fletcher is a retired professor who taught at England's University of East Anglia at Norwich. He has written several titles, including works covering Beckett, Claude Simon, and Robbe-Grillet.

Jack Murray is a professor emeritus at the University of California, Santa Barbara. He is the author of *The Landscapes of Alienation* and other titles.

Avi Sagi is a professor at Bar-Ilan University, Israel. He is the founder and director of a graduate program of hermeneutics at the university. He is also a senior research fellow at the Shalom Harman Institute in Jerusalem. He has published several titles, such as *Kierkegaard, Religion, and Existence*, and has edited many titles as well.

Robert C. Solomon was a professor at the University of Texas. He published more than forty books, including *Ethics and Excellence* and *The Joy of Philosophy*.

Acknowledgments

Jean-Paul Sartre, excerpts from *Literary and Philosophical Essays*, Annete Michelson (Translator): pp. 26–28, 41. London: Rider and Company, 1955. NY: Criterion, 1955. London: Hutchinson, 1968. Translated from Jean-Paul Sartre, *"Explication de l'étranger"* from *Situation* volume 1, © Editions Gallimard, 1947. Reprinted with permission.

R.W.B. Lewis, pages 68–71 and 299–302 from *The Picaresque Saint: Representative Figures in Contemporary Fiction*. Copyright © 1956, 1958 by R.W.B. Lewis. Reprinted by permission of HarperCollins Publishers and the Estate of R.W.B. Lewis.

Alain Robbe-Grillet, "Nature, Humanism, Tragedy" from *For a New Novel*. Translated by Richard Howard, pp. 62–64. Copyright © 1965 by Grove Press, Inc. Reprinted with permission from Grove/Atlantic, Inc. Originally published in French as *Pour un nouveau roman*. Copyright © 1963 by Les Editions de Minuit.

Patrick Henry, excerpts from *Voltaire and Camus: The Limits of Reason and the Awareness of Absurdity*, from *Studies on Voltaire and the Eighteenth Century*, edited by Theodore Besterman: pp. 249–252. © Theodore Besterman 1975. The Voltaire Foundation. By permission of the Voltaire Foundation, University of Oxford.

Brian T. Fitch, excerpt from *The Narcissistic Text: A Reading of Camus' Fiction*: pp. 55–57. © University of Toronto Press 1982. Reprinted with permission.

Patrick McCarthy, excerpt from *Albert Camus: The Stranger* by Patrick McCarthy: pp. 46–48. © Cambridge University Press 1988, 2004. Reprinted with the permission of Cambridge University Press.

Every effort has been made to contact the owners of copyrighted material and secure copyright permission. Articles appearing in this volume generally appear much as they did in their original publication with few or no editorial changes. In some cases, foreign language text has been removed from the original essay. Those interested in locating the original source will find the information cited above.

Index

Characters in literary works are indexed by first name (if any), followed by name of work in parentheses.